SO
YOU'RE
GOING TO
COLLEGE...

CONCERNS AND STRATEGIES FOR THE COLLEGE-BOUND

CHRISTOPHER WARREN

KILROY PRESS
Chapel Hill, N.C.

First Edition printing 1989
LC# 88-82123
ISBN# 0-9621001-0-2

Dedication

To those who played one role or many; for my enemies who motivated me beyond words, and for my friends and allies who kept me from becoming like my enemies.

Preface

In some measure, we all create our own realities. It is my sincere hope that you will find the following information both salient and useful in your career endeavors while you are involved in the more pressing and difficult task of becoming a person, and that you will become the happiest and healthiest individual it is possible for you to be in this troubled and polluted world. Every generation, like every wave on a shore, contributes something new to the sands of time on which they collectively make their imprint. What you make of what you've been left by those who have gone before you--for those who will follow you--can determine much of the future. Do not dismiss your possible contribution, for the grain of sand your seemingly meager efforts move may be the one that no one else was equipped or meant to change, and may make possible the jumblings of many other grains of sand that eventually amount to something, and that would not have been moved except for you jossling the first one. Go ahead and jossle the first one--yourself.

Acknowledgements

There are several people without whom this book would not have been possible, and they deserve special mention and thanks. They are:

My father, who allowed me to argue with him as I was growing up, instead of cutting off all debate as I'd seen other parents do. He listened and cared enough to debate with me, so that my critical acumen was developed.

My mother, who supported me in everything I did, and who took time to consider and care about how I was feeling in this life, aside from what I might or might not be achieving.

To those mentioned anonymously in the EXPERIENCES chapter, without your real life contributions this chapter and many of the ideas for this book would not have been possible.

David Williams, my High School English teacher, who realized I was bored in high school, and who encouraged me early on to study on my own by providing me with a suggested reading list which I first used before I developed my own.

To the support personnel in the computer labs on the University of North Carolina at Chapel Hill campus for their courteous and kind consideration during the writing of this book.

To two childhood friends, Kurt Dean and Jean Sagorski-Nagelkirk, who helped me see the difference between being spontaneous and being contrived by accepting me in the former mode during my childhood, formative years.

To my friends from the University of Michigan, Lester House people and other Big Chillers, who kept me sane, and gave me a place to be just myself in an often insane, non-self universitocosm.

To lovers past and present, without you it would have been no fun nor had any meaning at all.

To all those I have forgotten or whose contribution I was too preoccupied with myself to notice.

To myself, for making it happen.

TABLE OF CONTENTS

Introduction: Why I wrote this book?

Please, you say, not another how-to, self-help book about college--how to study, interview, get the job with the big fat paycheck, cope, have sex, have safe sex, get financial aid, start a business while in college, buy real estate, live with a roommate, choose a career... there are already too many suggestions for a reasonable person to handle, but if you have access (via the public library or $$$) to these books, look them over, you might get a few good ideas before you get confused.

What I have to offer is some simple, down to earth advice from me to you--that this world is full of people fighting each other, looking out for themselves, and you'd better become one of them or they are going to use you like so much cannon fodder for their own gain. Believe it. Altruism survives only in the realm of enlightened ideas, a place to visit after you have learned to fend for yourself, after you have carved out your own niche. Then you might be able to help a few people, but right now its You v.s. The World and all the smart money is backing the world. Understand?

This makes some cruel sense actually. Each of us is and should be our first responsibility. If you cannot or do not take care of yourself, you are not going to be able to take care of anyone else. However, many people out there have taken this sensible attitude to a new cutthroat, me-at-all-costs, competitive extreme. Get ready to live among them. All over that campus, in its finest traditions.

This book may seem like a combat manual for a reason-you are going to war. Your mission, if you decide to matriculate, is to recognize and defeat the enemy, use and aid your allies, and to reach your personal objectives.

Why Fight?

Life, it seems, is conflict, and conflict is primarily a result of struggling for survival, therefore one might first decide if one wishes to live. Facing this, we each decide to continue or forfeit, and make plans to further our individual decisions, our will to live tested daily by innumerable reasons to give up and pass to another, hopefully more satisfying, existence. Standard issue among these are:

> I SUFFER
> There is no love in this world.
> My life is meaningless.
> I'd be better off dead.
> Others would be better off if I were dead.
> I cannot get what I want in this world.
> I have lost that which I lived for.
> I have no reason or hope of a reason to live.
> Why not die?

Not being omniscient, I cannot confirm or deny the truth of any of these statements (except, perhaps for myself). All are statements of a present condition and tend to negate our memories of the past and prospects for the future. One must often be hopeful of better things to come and remember good times past in order to supplant current and reoccurring feelings of desperation and despair. Deciding to continue is an ongoing process, but once embarked upon seems to carry with it its own contagious, self-infecting determinism. We want to go on, and we find reasons to do so. Some take on a cause, others indulge hedonism and/or the pursuit of profit, and some find a simple satisfaction in their sense of self, or some combination thereof. Fortunately, idiosyncratic satisfactions abound. We choose to live, and this prospect holds forth struggle and inevitable conflict even for the most passive and nonviolent among us. Consider your methods and "weapons" carefully, and keep them prepared and ready, for you can expect to have use of them if you choose to survive and live in this world.

Why College?

Higher education can be the ticket to a more satisfying future, both monetarily and otherwise, though if not carefully purchased, that ticket can buy a ride to nowhere. One must know what one wants, and determine what it will take to reach each chosen destination(s). Take the time to look over all the "travel brochures" and talk to people who have been there, or still are there, before you buy that ticket. It is wise to do an internship, or seek employment in your chosen field before enlisting your efforts in that direction permanently. Be sure you really know and want all that will be implicit in your arriving at your chosen destination(s). Be as careful and thorough as you can about what you chose for the future because you might just get it.

Choosing Your Objectives

Your objective in college is to get the best possible grades, but do not confuse this with actual education. Much of what will make you effective in any future career will be learned outside the bonds of formal education. Therefore do not let school interfere.

There are many strategies besides "knowing everything" and "knowing almost everything" that lead to high grades; a sincere and burning interest in the topic is an excellent beginning even if the instruction is so obtuse or competition so undermining that personal interest is deadened. Other strategies range from a desire to excel, to developing razor keen study methods, to using Cliff notes, to virtuoso cheating. You will probably be witness to all, a practitioner of some, and hopefully not victimize yourself by choosing the latter.

Do not expect a complete, well-rounded formal education from college. Your personal effort and ability will largely determine your grades, but only your sense of curiosity and responsibility toward learning can complete your education. Use the library. Listen to touring speakers, drunks, fellow students, even professors--all those you are fortunate enough to hear. Live with people who are diverse and different from yourself and learn about them and from them. Seek out further reading in areas you've covered and found exciting in classes and explore any and all other interests discovered--above, beyond, and apart from the classroom. You might even take time off from school to do this. Develop a reading list. Learn from new experiences, people, and employment. By opening your mind in these and other ways, you decide how complete your education will become. Even in the mundane will be found tidbits of unmined usefulness and knowledge. You decide to look, and to keep looking even when it seems you are finding little. Do not depend on college courses alone to encompass useful knowledge. Depend on your own initiative and effort.

You will use the resources of the college or university, but much of your important work will be done outside the auspices of its direction. <u>Herein lies your real objective: your personal growth and development of a sense of self--you continuing to become the person you want to be--individually, interpersonally, spiritually, and careerwise--all in spite of the many obstacles in your path.</u> For better or worse there are millions of other young people enrolling in colleges and universities around the world, many as bright, ambitious and capable as you, who will be competing with you for those cherished positions that only a few can attain. Among them you will find allies and enemies and maybe a few friends, but all of them, either directly or indirectly, are competing with you for favored subsistence in this life, and though they be pleasant and polite in their pursuit, the inescapable fact is that some will win and others will lose. Life, at least in the academic and subsequent job market, is competition at its fiercest and not unlike nor less complex than an armed conflict or the cold war. Constantly shifting conditions at both the stated and covert levels exist, and those who adapt quickly and correctly will prosper. Welcome to the folly and the fray.

In this new arena, you are a beginner, a novice-irrevocably new meat. You can use this educational opportunity and in turn will be used by it, but in order to make the best of those resources in your present possession you must first know what you have, and second, what you want. There are many choices. You must choose daily between actions which may collectively determine your future chances of success or failure. Remember this.

On the other hand, you are a human being and may not always know exactly what you want. Be honest enough to admit to yourself that you don't know. If you lie to yourself or pretend to know when you do not, the actions you begin may become the pretext for you to live a lie or pretend to be something you are not for a very long difficult time, perhaps a lifetime. Not knowing is uncomfortable too, but can be amended by new experiences. You still may not completely know but you can know more about what you might like. Seek experiences that will help you define more clearly what you want. Only you can decide.

BASIC CONCERNS AND STRATEGIES
PART ONE: Tactical

Your first considerations should always be three basic requirements, Shelter, Food, and Clothing, in that order (unless your survival is in so much jeopardy that starvation is imminent, then obviously attaining food has priority). Individuals will desire different accoutrements, and here are some recommendations that are really more than recommendations, because if you falter here and cannot provide yourself with these basics to keep yourself healthy, you can forget about good grades, personal growth and any other pursuits involving a satisfying life.

Shelter: You need a place to live. As a freshperson, you will probably live in a dormitory and you may like it so much you will want to stay in university housing your entire college career. If not, or if a campus housing lottery could throw you out in the street, then after the first semester (or before if you think you can handle it), start thinking about housing for the next year. Look over the town. You want a safe, quiet, inexpensive, comfortable place, in that order. Why? Because-you need a safe and secure place, or real and/or imagined threats will destroy or undermine your efforts. Quiet will be necessary for serious study. Reasonable rent is highly desirable, not only if you are poor, but even if you are rich, since less rent paid out will help you stay solvent, and comfort is always an added plus. You also will want a place convenient to campus, a responsible and understanding landlord, and someone you can stand to live with for company and to share expenses. Or maybe you want to live alone. Or you might find a good arrangement with an elderly couple or single parent in town, your companionship and help around the house or with children in exchange for a reasonable rent--these can be wonderful learning experiences, but be careful these obligations do not demand too much of your time. Or you might manage an apartment complex for a free apartment, ditto the aforementioned concern about your time. Or, if you are handy, your parents might help you buy a house which you can fix up and live in and rent to other students, and possibly make a profit month to month or on resale after you graduate. Ditto the aforementioned concern about your time. Start looking early. Find a place that makes you happy, a place you can look forward to coming home to during the midterm crunch after someone has just stolen your backpack with all your notes and extra money in it. Other options are available, such as rushing the Greek system (this can be a good place to live, but, depending on which campus and which system, can be limiting in other ways--almost everyone who lives there is of wealthy parentage, white, subtly racist, attractive, somewhat verbal, in business school, trendy, "selected" by their peers via their heritage, appearance, normalcy or general blandness, and because they are so status quo, though there are exceptions, usually about as interesting and stimulating as a fifty pound bag of fertilizer), or cooperative housing if available on your campus (a more diverse option people-wise, and anyone who is willing to share the work can join).

Food: Develop a monthly budget for food. Healthy, simple, easy-to-prepare food. Check out available nutritional guides and cookbooks recommended for college students. Eat out, if you can, once or twice a week. Splurge some, but do not blow your budget. If you live in a dormitory and food service is provided, try not to overindulge yourself on sweets--food is not a substitute for an exciting, engaging life. Also, try to vary your diet within the constraints of what's offered, get enough from the four basic food groups, dairy, bread and grains, fruits and vegetables, meat and poultry, and other protein sources, like beans and rice (very good if you find yourself suddenly or endlessly on a limited budget). College is a great time to experiment with ethnic dishes, especially if the ethnic food you are interested in has a flesh and blood person available who knows how to prepare it or a good place where it is served. Alternative diets associated with different religions, such as various forms of vegetarianism, can also be explored after you get out of the dormitory and begin to live off campus (though I've heard rumors that some college food services are offering a phantasmagoric selection of foods). At present, dieticians and nutritionists are recommending a diet rich in complex carbohydrates, without excess protein and low in fats, especially saturated fat which increases the cholesterol level in the body, and causes plague deposits on artery walls which lead to vascular problems and heart disease. Read some books about food and healthy diets. Listen to your body, what does it want that's good for you? Take care of yourself by learning to nourish yourself right---nobody else will.

Clothing: You can wear whatever you want at your new home away from home and among your friends, but in any situation where there is a doubt in your mind about what might be appropriate---wear something appropriate. On most campuses, unless there is a strict dress code, most anything will pass, however some people in the academic community may be sensitive to appearance, and may make judgements about you based on your appearance. Yes, this is unfair, infantile, and denies your uniqueness and creativity as a person, especially if you possess obvious great taste and have decided to become your own personal fashion designer, but the fact remains that your appearance, if too alien to a person you are interacting with, can become a distraction, and interfere with your ultimate purpose in communicating with them. As will be mentioned later, appearance and appropriate demeanor can be a potent weapon in furthering your interests. Perhaps directing your energies into what is on the cutting edge of appropriate can satiate your creative energies. If money for clothes is a problem, simply do your best. Obvious poverty made the best of, along with clean thoughts and good manners, can be useful social impressions, and if you are stuck with this financial constraint, there are ways to turn this to advantage.

PART TWO: PSYCHOLOGICAL STRATEGY

It is basic to success in any conflict situation that one maintain a personal sense of inward order. You may have heard older people say," well, they can't take that away from you" about one thing or another that they felt gave them irrevocable security, such as wealth, or property, or a college degree, or a pension. The sad fact is that these and almost everything else can be taken from an individual. However, if that individual, though stripped of all worldly security, is still of sound mind, he or she can still possess patience, calmness, and the ability to deliberate and create solutions---all qualities that contribute to climbing out of whatever hole fate or one's own actions or a combination thereof have throw one into. *What you are inwardly, aside from your personal attractiveness and outward beauty, or any corporeal thing you possess, or any powerful people who favor you: this is what will determine your winning or losing in the long term.* For this reason, it is important to begin to explore and maintain one's inward self.

Unfortunately, nobody can tell you exactly how to do this, though some authors will give you a detailed explanation and exercise as to exactly how you should go about it. Fortunately or unfortunately, their furious scribblings cannot be all things to all people, and though I am sure they help many, they may hurt some with their necessarily condensed, encapsulated thinking. Feel free to disagree responsibly, for in the final analysis, even with a conscientious guide, all decisions are yours. The best I can offer is to encourage you to think about yourself, how you are feeling, what you are thinking, and then step back from this, accept it, perceive it, and ask yourself what you think and feel about it. Keep recycling this process. Read some good literature, or psychoanalytic works (or anything else) and compare the author's observations about human nature (or anything else) with your observations of yourself (or anything else). This is a lifelong process, but the goal here is to define your objectives by knowing (now) what you have and what you want for the future. You can only realize this by knowing yourself.

Consider the following parameters:

Time: The one common denominator for all human beings---we each are given the same portion in each twenty-four hour day. What will you do with yours today and why? What do you want to be doing with your time three years, five years, ten years from now? Much of this will be determined by what you do today. Perhaps you should consider this once in awhile, maybe even once a week. Reflect (steps 1-3)---where????? have I been, where????? am I now, where????? do I want to go. Even go so far as to write it down or tape record it, any and all thoughts and feelings, so you can remember how your decisions have evolved and note any underlying and/or recurring patterns.

You: What is unique about you inwardly? What does nobody else know about you, but you---your dreams, feelings, ideas. The one person in this life you have the greatest likelihood and the best opportunity to know, love, have sexual experiences with, learn from, create with, and enjoy to the fullest is you and you alone. Relish yourself. Tell the truth(s) to yourself: about yourself and everything else. If you are fortunate, you may find others to share with, but this does not always happen to the extent nor depth we desire, and if it does, then you cannot be better prepared for it than to have a thorough understanding of yourself.

Chance: The luck of the draw, a throw of the dice, the passing opportunities that life seems to cast across our bows, they come in many forms: traveling to new places (like college), people we meet, new ideas or new understanding of old ones, or new ways of seeing the world. Sometimes we see, sometimes not. Be aware, open your mind to emerging possibilities you may not have considered and be sure to investigate them. You may find something valuable and important that has been overlooked.

Balance: Be human. You are not a machine that can run nonstop, ever-throttling forward toward greater production. You are a human being, you will become tired, sometime you must rest. And play. And dream. And procrastinate. And ponder the imponderable. And be undecided. And laugh, and love, and lay in the sun. Only then can you return to work refreshed and recharged enough to take the next hill and to seek your objectives. Sometimes you will work hard and long, and rest little, other times the tasks ahead will be more gradual. Even in the heat of battle or unrelenting pressure of a deadline there is time for a short break, a joke, a laugh. Strike a balance between work and other important things.

Reflect and consider these opinions when confused and see how you relate to them. This may be a difficult task as your attention is swept away by the many attractions of college life. Warrior-types may find these considerations too soft and disarming: unto them I say---ignore these considerations at your own peril. Without a core, a known self to strike forth from, even the most able students will likely find themselves awash in choices, and will repeatedly misdirect their energies. Know that the first and only weapon in your arsenal is you, and what you can create. Realize you will not always know exactly what you want---try new things, explore new interests and ideas, buy time and keep your options open until you think you know what you want. If you make a mistake and decide when you really don't know, realize it, step back, make the best of what you have, and begin again. Persevere. Remember---this is competition and conflict, a war zone you enter as a novice, full of people as devastating to your evolving objectives and career plans as land mines and bullets---they can and will delay you, stop you, make you fall short of or even prevent you from reaching your goals, both daily and in the long term. You must learn how to prepare yourself for their contingencies, but first you must learn how to recognize the enemy.

SUMMARY OF BASIC CONCERNS AND STRATEGIES

PART ONE: TACTICAL

Provide yourself with the following in the order given:

    1) A safe, quiet, inexpensive, comfortable shelter.

    2) A healthy variety of food.

    3) Appropriate, but self-expressing clothing.

PART TWO: PSYCHOLOGICAL STRATEGY

Know what you are today. Determine what you have and what you want by being cognizant of how you do the following each day.

        1) Use your time.

        2) Value and explore yourself.

        3) Be aware.

        4) Find balance in life.

Recommendation--keep a personal diary or journal of this information, any and all stray thoughts and feelings, for future planning purposes.

RECOGNIZING THE ENEMY

As cynical as this may sound, it is not an unrealistic proposition to suppose that few people you will meet in this world have your best interest at heart, and even fewer still sincerely care about what happens to you and shed tears or raise prayers upon your demise. Perhaps with this in mind, it may not be so hard to believe that some people in this world could be classified as your bona-fide enemy. Granted, it is not fruitful to daily be casting suspicious eyes at all who cross your path, always looking for the least provocation to justify your predisposition, but the maxim," Fool me once, shame on you, fool me twice, shame on me," is not too paranoid an attitude to consider bringing into actual practice. Certainly, I have been fooled more than once by situations and people at college who should not have fooled me at all, and it is my hope that you can recognize and avoid some of these difficulties by considering earlier than I did the potential for certain situation and/or persons to be hazardous to you fulfilling your objectives.

The following people have the potential to be your enemy:

Admission, and administrative officials, secretaries, professors, other students in your classes, roommates, housemates, campus police, drug using friends, "friends" who change on you, landlords, employers, psychoanalysts, psychologists, counselors, advisors, clergy, parents, and even yourself.

In short, -ANYONE-can be a potential enemy. An "enemy" is anyone or anything that prevents or hinders you from realizing your objective(s). Things that could be the enemy are:

Anything that costs money, like housing, tuition, food, clothing, repairs, recreation; addictive drugs, like alcohol, marijuana, speed, cocaine; any breakdownable mechanical device you depend on, like an auto, calculator, computer, air conditioner, electric heater, moped, or bicycle.

Only through recognizing the potential for each of these things and people to present a problem and what the nature of the problem might be and how you might begin to solve the problem-only then will you have succeeded in recognizing the enemy. In later chapters we will cover some particulars of selected cases, but even in those explanations I have not tried nor do I believe I can be expect to cover all and every possible contingency. In general, ala Murphy's law, if it can happen, it will. And if you can imagine it happening, it might happen. To a greater extent than you might now realize, your ability to perceive people and situations, and imagine their many possible behaviors and outcomes will greatly influence your success or failure in upcoming encounters.

Because of this, whenever ungermane I have purposely avoided generating stereotypes of different people who might be enemies. Both self-help books and popular media have found it useful and profitable to stereotype campus life and its participants into easily definable and recognizable groups. Most stereotypes are created and become popular because the stereotyped individual(s) does in fact possess some of the traits attributed, usually in a superficial way, and the stereotype suits the purposes of those who created it and believe in it. Some suppose that various "types" theories serve a useful purpose, that they provide us with an immediately accessible character sketch of a new person by virtue of any number of easily observable factors such as role, race, creed, gender or occupation: no matter how limiting or erroneous. Others offer types as convenient starting points, a place to be comfortable with someone you can pretend to know until you really get to know them--if you ever do. Both theories have their genesis in the generous investment it takes to marshall the time and effort to observe and reflect on another person in order to come to know them.

The greatest hazard in stereotyping people is the danger of oversight, of not seeing beneath the outward constraints of the assumption, and missing traits that do not fit or even directly contradict the stereotype. The absent-minded professor of Walt Disney fame was not completely nor always absent-minded, and jocks sometimes have brains and are really earning the excellent grades they receive. On the other hand, do not miss the superficial information stereotypes have to offer that may be useful, if only sometimes erroneous, such as that premeds are really very competitive, and preppies really do like cotton mesh shirts (like everyone else).

My purpose in avoiding the use of stereotypes whenever possible is directed towards encouraging you to make your own observations about potential enemies (and allies to be mentioned directly), and to create your own "types" when useful and to keep their ledgers up to date and open.

Try to remember, even after you have registered a certain person as an enemy, that they live in the same competitive world you do, and may not be doing what they are doing to you out of dislike or malice towards you, but because their interpretation of the competitive situation and/or other factors sanction their behavior. You want to act in self-defense only, to avoid the thrust of their inconsideration without becoming vindictive. It is seldom worth it, figuratively or literally, to plot their demise in some drastic fashion, you acting to deliver some kind of definitive kill shot. Fantasize about this if it helps you deal with your anger, but you stray from the intentions of this book and the strategies to be ascribed for such difficult situations if you choose to do so.

RECOGNIZING AN ALLY

Just as there are people and things that can be "enemies," there are also "allies." ANYONE who helps you realize your objectives is an ally. This distinction between enemies and allies is easy enough to see, but becomes less clear when placed in the context of human behavior. A person who acts as your enemy now can be your ally in the future. It is the action that each person manifests that is important. A person can be your ally and enemy in the same sentence, and it will be up to you to dissect and discern the various meanings of actions observed, but in general, individuals are not this variable; either the individual will be your enemy or ally, and rarely will they change over in any highly significant way. However it is possible, and some examples will be illustrated in the EXPERIENCES chapter, but first a word about what seasonings (besides a grain of salt) that I would like you to sprinkle about and ingest as you digest the following distinctions.

Look upon what you read here much like you might an experience of learning musical composition and/or martial arts. A teacher of musical composition would give you bars, staffs, key signatures, chords, inversions and progressions, advice on what instruments set what mood--all the tools you would need to compose your own music. The martial arts instructor would give you kicks and blows, vulnerable points on an attacker's body, and exercises to help you integrate all the movements---but in battle, as in musical composition, it is you who will have to decide how to use the tools provided. I am giving you tools also, paradigms to look at college life through, both as a wonderful creative possibility and as a fierce battle and still altogether a fine art, but it will be up to you to compose the cerebral music that determines how you will fare in the battle of the campus. You will throw no blows, but your concerted, orchestrated actions will involve some psychological thrust and parry, and will be more effective than any physical strike-but first some further distinctions.

QUALITIES OF ENEMIES AND ALLIES

Enemies	**Allies**
indifferent	truthful
burned out	responsible
uncaring	caring
dishonest	straightforward
two-faced	personable
self-hating	respectful
Without thought of your	self-loving
needs	lovable
Tell destructive half-truths	prompt
Change things without	There when you need them
thinking how it will affect	Mindful of your needs
you	Supportive of you
Exploitive of you	Reinforce your self-
Undermine your self-	confidence
confidence	Keep promises
Double-talker	Therapeutic and healing
Directly or indirectly	Help clarify your choices
threatens your health or well-	Have reasonable stated
being	expectations.
Want to control you	
Do not keep promises	
Attack your spirit, ideas, or	
initiative ad hominem	

Enemy or Ally?

You now have some idea of the wide scope of who may be potential enemies and allies, what criteria define each and what kind of traits they are likely to present. In later chapters, I will try to show you where to look for enemies and allies in your daily interactions. As the author, I can draw these distinctions, list traits and will give examples in later chapters, but I cannot endow you with the judgement to recognize exactly how and when someone has become your enemy or ally. I admit the distinction is simplistic, though I hope you will agree after you have finished reading this book, that it is pragmatic, and that it can be used to understand and analyze situations, and provide insights that can defuse threatening situations and profit you in your struggle to reach your objectives. The important thing to realize is that you recognize the potential for a particular action by another to give you difficulty or advantage, and that you take steps to minimize their negative impacts, or allow their favor, respectively. There will be times where you can make the best of it, and other times when it is best to retreat to fight another day, or put your efforts into another front. Consider each situation separately and carefully. You are on your own.

ADVANCED CONCERNS AND STRATEGIES

We will involve ourselves with the following constellation:

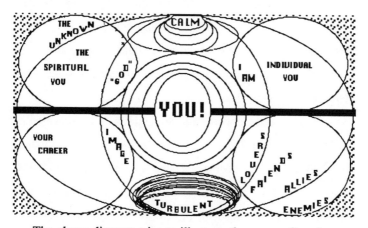

The above diagram tries to illustrate the energy flow between salient divisions of self for explanation purposes only. The actual patterns that exists are perhaps beyond our comprehension, or at least beyond the scope of my ability to diagram. In Basic Concerns and Strategies I tried to emphasize and encompass some basic tactical considerations and the first certain and ongoing relationship any **YOU!** has, that between you and **I AM** or your individual self. Second, and as an adjunct to this first relationship, there is the relationship to the unknown, or "God" if you wish to call it--the relationship between you and your spiritual self. These two interactions take place inwardly, in the relative peace and calm of introspection (above the solid horizontal line), an exercise made so by our insight into and greater control over its pace, agenda, and function in our lives. The other two interactions; between you and your career, and you and other people occur outside this peaceful realm, in the turbulent world of exospection (below the solid horizontal line), where our individual control and insight is comparatively diminished. Both "worlds" involve other people and things, and the flow of interactions probably bears limited similarity to any thick or thin lines I could draw, though I believe if I did draw lines, all parts would have connections to all others, and the thickness or thinness of each line would perhaps be different for each individual.

View Advanced Concerns and Strategies as a continuation of Basic Concerns and Strategies. If skills and habits of thought introduced in Basic Concerns and Strategies are underdeveloped, atrophied, or lacking, benefit from Advanced Concerns and Strategies will be diminished. In addition to those introduced in Basic Concerns and Strategies, reflect and consider the following new parameters (and record your thoughts and feeling in some permanent way, such as a diary, journal, or tape recording):

Your Spiritual Self: This relationship has to do with how you explain things to yourself that you do not know, cannot know, and do not understand. Thoughts like," Why am I here?" and "Is there a God?," and "What is the origin of all things in the universe?" reside here early and questions of scientific fact, creative possibility and further self-knowledge may come later. This is your relationship with the unknown and like so many other relationships in this life, there are so very many things you can do with it. Only you can decide.

You could become involved in an organized religion. Most people do. Religions in general have many things in common; a concept of a deity, recommendations for how to live a life worthy of the deity, a theory of creation, worship services with various rites of passage and rituals, and predictions about what lies beyond this life to mention only a few. Study several religions and realize their similarities and differences, their historical basis, and their ways of worship. Most will leave you with far more questions than answers, and perhaps this is the way it should be. Understanding of your own chosen religion cannot help but be heightened by this type of investigation. However, there is the chance that as you accumulate questions and unsatisfying answers, your faith in your chosen religion and religions in general will begin to wane. You could "fall so far" as they say, that you become an atheist, one who believes there is no God or that God is dead, or an agnostic, one who does not deny God, but denies the possibility of knowing him/her; or you could move in the opposite direction and become a member of the clergy, your faith deepened by thorough examination. It all depends on what happens to your faith via the religious teachings you experience. Faith, as it interfaces with knowing or not knowing the unknowable, can be defined as thinking that one does know the unknown through the predilectitory beliefs of one's faith, or that one does not and cannot know the unknowable, but that one trusts some benevolent, omnipotent, omniscient force in the universe that does know--and that this force works in strange and mysterious ways beyond our comprehension for our overall betterment. And then there is the question of free will, determinism and indeterminism, does God decide all or does he invite us to come his way, and hope that we do, but leave our path a choice for each of us to confront? What your attitude and answer is to this and any other questions poised by my previous exposition is what interacting with your spiritual self is all about.

My emphasis here is not on what you decide, but that you be cognizant of your thoughts about unknowns and consider them, because how you interact with the unknown can affect other important interactions diagramed above. Many great and useful discoveries were products of how humans have interacted with unknowns. If Copernicus had either accepted or ignored the then current religious view of the physical universe and not sought a further, more satisfying explanation, humankind might still believe their home planet to be the center of the universe. Jet engines would not crisscross the nation everyday if nobody had faith in the idea that man could fly. Word processors would be things of dreams instead of actual reality, and one would not be responding to my touch at this very moment.

Consider an example closer to home. Many men and women have endured abysmal marriages because their religions prohibit divorce. Think of someone you know who seems happier after their divorce or the divorce of their parents, and you may know why I call on you to not blindly accept or completely ignore your uncertainties, whether they be personal or worldly. Confront them, tangle with them, enlist books and knowledgeable people to help you, use the questions they generate to create, but do not blindly accept or completely ignore the issue. Examine the problem, know why you do believe or do not believe, and what it is in the explanation that buttresses your faith or is too questionable for you to rely upon, and question your conclusions. The discoveries you reap in your confrontations with unknowns may be more important than you realize.

Choice of Career: First of all, you must have the ability to do it, next, it is best to enjoy it, and lastly, with all its ups and downs, do you LOVE it and can this love endure? Or could and should you do it just for the money?

Ultimately, you must choose something, but every choice you make does not have to be final. In your choice of college courses, keep your options open, but more importantly, keep your mind open to the possibility that you may end up wanting to do a job that at present seems totally unrelated to anything you are doing now. Chemistry majors do end up corporate attorneys, plumbers, and comedians, and find happiness in these careers. Because there are so many possibilities out there, and it is unlikely that you have only one talent or one thing that you could enjoy and love, it is most important that you do a patient, thorough, and ongoing examination of those possibilities mentioned in Basic Concerns and Strategies in regards exploring and knowing yourself and your talents.

Of course, their are practical considerations to sort as well. Will this career allow me to earn enough money to live and keep myself and any significant others in the style that I and they could become accustom too? Will there be adequate jobs in my chosen field so that I won't have to face the spectre of unemployment in the future? Could my chosen field become obsolete? What are the prospects for advancement? If I find that I do not enjoy this career ten years from now, will there be other possible offshoots that I could enjoy, or another career that my degree might qualify me or nearly qualify me for?

Many of these questions confront unknowns, and you ignore them at your own risk--try to consider future possibilities, both positive and negative. Before you commit yourself to a career path and the necessary coursework, I suggest you do an internship or seek a work experience in or as near as possible to the actual job that you believe you would like. Talk to people who are doing this job, and most importantly, talk with people who have left this job for greener pastures. Decide if you can do it, if you will enjoy it, and if you love it enough that your love for it will endure. Then, after all this, go get it, and do not be deterred by the seemingly endless and devastating setbacks that will inevitably crop up. Desist only if you discover you do not really want it, not because the path to it becomes difficult (compare and contrast this directive with another underlined one on p.14 of Basic Concerns and Strategies).

Should You Be At College?

Heretofore you have completed the reading of Basic and Advanced Concerns and Strategies in preparation for the academic struggle ahead. Only you can decide if you have completed enough of the thinking that must be done in order for the reading to be useful. If you do not feel secure with the thoughts and feelings you have generated, and have not delineated at least some of the things you want as regards a future direction(s), then perhaps you should consider not beginning or continuing your college education at present. There will be frugal choices of time and money ahead and if you try to continue without completing your thinking on these considerations in some significant measure, I fear you will become disillusioned and more confused, and your time and effort at college will be wasted.

This does not mean you should not attend college or leave campus--depending on your special circumstances. If you are a freshperson, either just starting or a semester into your college career, you may have any number of required, general courses that you can throw your energies into and complete, so that you will have these nuisance tasks behind you when you do decide on a direction. Meanwhile, you can still actively search your options while on campus; either through employment or volunteering in a possible areas of interest, or sitting in on some advanced courses, or just by interacting with new and interesting people. Possibly limit the boring, general courses to part-time status so that you have more time for the important process of searching, because after you get on a tack toward a career, your time for fun, friends, lovers, and extended travel adventures will become more limited, so now is the time for these things along with your searching, if you can afford them financially. Do not waste your youth. A year or so of indecision filled with the aforementioned things is probably one of the best experiences that can happen to you. Do not forget, however, that along with this comes the responsibility to eventually make some decisions, to continue searching, and ultimately get on with your life. Youth does not last forever, and though it should be enjoy while it is here, preparation for when it fades and interests change, or for when it is forcible taken away by the society we live in, must be made or the consequences suffered.

Suppose you just do not want to take any courses. Should you leave campus? You could get a job, read some things on your own, and do some of the things I mentioned above, but perhaps your life and desires lie elsewhere. There are many satisfying careers that do not require college, but usually demand some kind of training. Reconsider the parameters of Basic and Advanced Concerns and Strategies, and decide what you want, and if you think what you want is not on campus, but somewhere else--go there. You can always return, and you can always leave again. Only you can decide.

There again is that fine line--knowing what you want. Sometimes you will know what you want and won't be able to get it immediately. Have patience, keep and refine your desire, if it slips away, perhaps you did not want it as badly as you thought. Have financial priorities, a required textbook is more important that another record album. Time allocations may be especially demanding--that soap opera, or evening television show, or special date or activity might not fit into your schedule of other responsibilities. Knowing when you are sure of your goal and when to advance is as important as knowing when your goal is currently unreachable or not what you really want. One who retreats correctly, keeping what has already been gained intact, can return to engage the problem another day. Know when to retreat as well as when to advance.

Whether you decide to retreat or advance as far as your college enrollment is concerned, here is one further tactical consideration to be aware of:

Stress: What is stress? One comical explanation is that stress is the effort it takes to refrain from giving a sound beating to every inconsiderate fool you meet who so richly deserves it. Everyone evolves different means for dealing with stress, some healthy, others not so habilitating. Regular exercise, besides being good for you in general, is an excellent method for rejuvenating one's body as well as one's attitude. Try to chose something you can do on a regular basis, some 2-4 times a week (check with a physician if you experience pain in these efforts, or have any limiting health problems), and be sure to chose something you enjoy doing, even though it requires effort.

Sometimes these two requirements of regularity and enjoyment will come into conflict, in that what you enjoy is difficult to do regularly, or what is not enjoyable is easily available. As example, you may enjoy a team sport, but find it difficult to get enough other players together for a game on a regular basis, so you end up doing something not as enjoyable, but easily assessable, like jogging or swimming. Predictables, like weather, availability of facilities, and being sure you can always get an adequate workout are other factors to consider.

Another good way to alleviate stress is by planning a cool-out period everyday, a time when you relax and put away your daily cares for an extended period of time. This can be as simple as just rocking on a front porch for twenty minutes, or a walk in a garden alone, or can become as involved as learning a form of meditation. Whatever form a cool-out period takes, try to reserve a quiet time alone for yourself each day, a time to forget the day's responsibilities for a brief time and let silence and effortlessness become part of your existence. Be nice to yourself.

This completes Advanced Concerns and Strategies.

SUMMARY OF ADVANCED CONCERNS AND STRATEGIES

Spiritual Self

1) Be willing to ask questions that do not have answers.

2) Realize the content of these questions and their possible importance.

3) Accept and confront these unknowns.

4) Create from this synthesis.

Choice of Career-To Know Thyself

1) Have the ability to do it.

2) Enjoy doing it.

3) Love doing it, and have a feeling this love will endure.

4) A satisfactory match as regards:

Money

Lifestyle

Future employment

Advancement

5) Good future offshoot potential for a different, but similar career.

6) Internship or other experience to reinforce your judgement.

7) Knowing that this is what you want despite inevitable setbacks.

Stress

1) Awareness of its affects on you.

2) Exercise to alleviate its affects.

3) Quiet time to empty one of its causes.

At this point, it is assumed that the reader has completed Basic and Advanced Concerns and Strategies to the extent that he or she will elect to continue or matriculate in college, and that a sensitized or new attention to one's sense of self has developed and is continuing to evolve. This sense of self includes reflections on core issues highlighted in Basic Concerns and Strategies and those that lie in the comparative calm of the Advanced Concerns and Strategies Constellation, such as personal identity, idiosyncrasies, and attitude toward the unknowns of life. Decisions about career to the extent that one has decided to explore a limited number of areas, and then make further decisions is all that is hoped for at this time.

The rest of this book will be devoted to Special Concerns and Strategies for use in actual college situations. It is especially important at this time, though of some relative importance when considering the Advanced Concerns and Strategies Constellation, that readers consider the difference between simple linear thinking and more complex constellational thinking. Briefly, linear thinking involves moving from concept to concept, point to point, to arrive at a single conclusion; while constellational thinking may involve many levels. Several point to point transitions may be taking place in constellational thinking so that one may see the whole; or groups of points may become one or one become many-- all to a single or multiple conclusion. The essential difference between the two types of thinking is that while linear thinking holds and is aware of only one truth at a time, constellational thinking may hold and be aware of several, sometimes partially conflicting truths at one time. The challenge of constellational thinking is the synthesis of workable conclusions which are useful only with continued awareness of multiple truths and probabilities. Much of the application of Special Concerns and Strategies will involve the learning and application of constellational thinking, as well as thorough linear analysis.

One last preface and caution about Special Concerns and Strategies. It is my belief that some mastery of these concepts will contribute to your college success, however, do not expect these ideas or the practice thereof to be without some initial psychological incongruences. For the purposes described in Special Concerns and Strategies, some individuals will find it difficult to become less than completely and utterly themselves all of the time; the thespian-like nature of being in control of oneself confused with being a fraud. They will find their sense of self so moralistically or otherwise keenly developed and in command, or have unrealistic ideas about what they can change in this world or in people they meet, that they will be unable to selectively present themselves so as to further their best interest and/or defuse difficult or potentially harmful situations. For them, I will not argue the morality of my recommendations, but only their effectiveness, it being my contention that their refusal to adapt to prevailing conditions may keep them from achieving much of what their developing selves would like to and could become, and that their reluctance may ultimately affect the very survival of both themselves and those they care about. Others will develop ways to live with these seeming dichotomies in varying degrees, and will survive and prosper. Still others who have not developed any sense of self will find the instructions easy to follow and instigate, becoming consummate social actors and actresses to the near exclusion of all else within themselves. They may appear to prosper as judged by materialistic standards, but will be without any sense of success or failure for lack of direction in knowing what they want, possibly lost in the trappings of power for power's sake, and ultimately finding themselves-one terrible day-without joy and wonderment as a human being for lack of attention to an essential core element of their existence--a sense of self.

INTRODUCTION TO SPECIAL CONCERNS AND STRATEGIES

Rules of Special Concerns and Strategies

1) Never sacrifice your sense of self.
2) Accept and understand the power curve.
3) Accept the sole objective of striving to achieve best grades possible.
4) Do what is necessary to fulfill Rule No. 3.

Those who chose to follow these prescriptions should continue exercises mentioned in Basic and Advanced Concerns and Strategies. A journal, diary, or tape recorded record of continued Basic and Advanced Concerns and Strategies issues is strongly recommended for references purposes. Wholly separate and apart from this, begin a Special Concerns and Strategies notebook. Its use will become evident.

A reiterary note on striving for the best grades possible--do not be so naive as to confuse this with actual education. Good grades are an indication that the recipient was able to marshall enough intelligence and discipline over a semester's time to meet someone else's expectations and measure for adequate command of topic as presented, and to merit a certain ranking. The focus of this demanded regurgitation of knowledge and subsequent measure of achievement is necessarily narrowing, and may not be an adequate measure of the person's actual ability and knowledge in the area. What most high grades amount to is the most correct answers on tests and sometimes an instructor's subjective judgement of your arguments and ability. Do not confuse your knowledge of an area with the grade received. You may know much more, and in some cases, much less. Do not connect grades with self-esteem, allowing your current level of achievement to determine how you feel about yourself. Granted, you will feel elated when things go your way, and disappointed when they do not, but try, as Kipling says, to "treat these two imposters just the same" or at least temper your swings of mood with realistic evaluation. Are you really as smart or as stupid as that single letter grade is suppose to indicate? Chances are you are not; in either case.

Instead, indulge and cultivate a habit of self-evaluation. Knowing about one's far-reaching interest in a topic and what one's current level of knowledge is are far more important things to know than "what someone else thought about how much they thought you were suppose to know about what you knew." Take test grades and other teacher evaluation as means to help evaluate yourself. Upon the return of essays and term papers, take the criticism on a paper for what its worth, use it to write better, or to write a better paper for this particular reviewer. Shed no tears over wrong answers on tests that you either realize are wrong and why immediately, or can understand why they are wrong with explanation, or that asks such a picky question, that you can only narrow it down to two possibilities and can remember where it was written in a textbook, but cannot quite remember enough to answer the question correctly--this stuff is not worth committing to memory, you can look it up if you need to know, since you know

SPECIAL CONCERNS AND STRATEGIES
Lesson One: The Power Curve

Special Concerns and Strategies assumes you are a freshperson who has just matriculated into college. The following power curve is not complete for all relationships and interactions possible, and you will have to realize and construct your own impressions into a power curve for your particular situation(s). The point is to realize who holds what ultimate power, or how the balance of power rests or interfaces between many. In general the following overall picture concerning assumptions of hierarchy i.e., the power curve on campus are accurate:

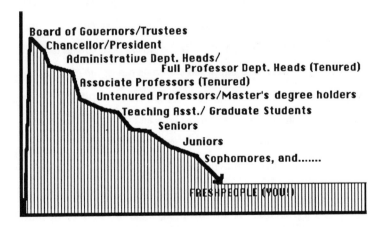

Board of Governors/Trustees
Chancellor/President
Administrative Dept. Heads/
    Full Professor Dept. Heads (Tenured)
Associate Professors (Tenured)
    Untenured Professors/Master's degree holders
    Teaching Asst./ Graduate Students
    Seniors
    Juniors
    Sophomores, and.......
FRESHPEOPLE (YOU!)

In each microcosmic situation you will encounter there will be mini-hierarchies that you should become aware of that are either subsets of the above or completely separate from it. Generally, either as an undergraduate student or freshperson, you will most likely be at or near the bottom of each hierarchy you encounter.

Do not despair. Each position in a power curve has its advantages, liabilities, and responsibilities, and each needs the others to complete the functioning of the hierarchy. Those at the top need those at the bottom to have someone to be on top of and to give them function and purpose in having someone to serve. Those at the bottom need those at the top to help them climb up from the bottom. Each in turn used others and is used by them. You are at the bottom, but those above you need you. Problematic for you is the fact that there are many others just like you who could meet their needs, but if you meet their basic requirements it is much less work for them to work with you and keep you around, rather than having to recruit and indoctrinate someone new. Their job is to serve you, for which you pay often inflated tuitions and fees that they would often prefer to forget you paid, and believe that they are providing you with their supposed expertise out of the goodness of their hearts when the relationship is really better described as fee for service--they are thinking of your welfare and learning experience in some cases, but invariably they will be thinking about their pocketbooks as well. Let them believe they are serving you out of their magnanimousness, making you a better person overall, and doing you a priceless good turn. Many qualities may be in short supply among those administrators, professors, and others you meet, but ego will not be among them. Outplaying them at their own game is possible.

It is important that you, as early as possible, begin to gather the following information and construct each mini-hierarchy you inevitably become involved in:

1) Who is in the hierarchy?

2) Who has the absolute power, or if power is shared, how is it shared and who holds the most influence?

3) What are the responsibilities of each person in the hierarchy, and how do these responsibilities mesh and interact?

4) Where you are in the hierarchy, and what pressure points you can push via meeting your responsibilities or legitimately pressing others to meet theirs so as to manipulate the situation to your advantage?

EXAMPLES OF HIERARCHIES

Professor Luke teaches Biology 100 with help from Teaching Assistants John, Paul, and Mary. Besides the use of hired test graders, these are the only persons besides you and your fellow students in this hierarchy. Professor Luke holds almost all the power, but his Teaching Assistants, who are also graduate students, have some influence, this varying with each assistant. Professor Luke is responsible for general presentation, the Teaching Assistants expand on this, and answer specific questions left unclear or unanswered by Professor Luke. The miscellaneous graders evaluate tests and quizzes per Professor Luke's instructions. This hierarchy looks like this:

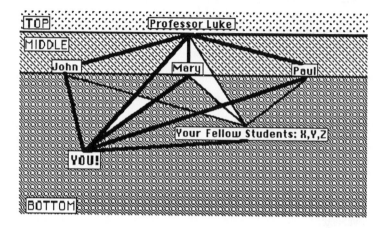

All parties are able to communicate with each other, each from their respective power level. As your enrollment at college stretches past the first semester, there will evolve a list of students that you come to know or have known from previous classes, and you can keep this list under "Your Fellow Students--X,Y,Z, etc." This completes the basic construction of this hierarchy.

The above is an example of the average hierarchical complexity of most classes you will encounter. The most simple will be:

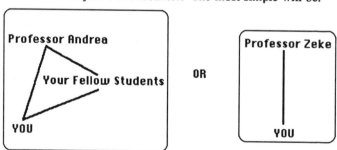

In these hierarchies, the professors have nearly absolute power, while you and your fellow students have limited influence. Of course, there are appeal committees, and heads of departments above professors (you might want to include them and a general understanding of their various powers in your construction of the hierarchy by attaining a copy of their procedures), and sometimes you can improve your grade or other conditions through their influence, but within the time frame of the semester, the professor is in control. Going over the professor's head may get you branded as a troublemaker. Do so only if the issue is important enough to expend the effort and risk the stigma. The further focuses of Special Concerns and Strategies will be confined to the nexus of relationships in these mini-hierarchies.

PRESSURE POINTS

If you could manipulate your parents, and/or your brothers and sisters as a child, then you can learn to manipulate a hierarchy. The entire process starts with your dissatisfaction with something and wanting to change it. First you locate the executor of the problem, and usually, if previous experience has not taught you that this is futile, you approach this person first. If this has no effect, you can call on other people in the web of the hierarchy to help you put pressure on the executor of the problem.

In a hierarchy, this pressure can be generated from the bottom up or from the top down. Most vulnerable are those caught in the middle who are trying to please naturally conflicting points of view, like the Teaching Assistants in the Biology 100 hierarchy.

They can be worked on from multiple pressure points via you, your fellow students, and the professor. However all members of a hierarchy are vulnerable in one way or another.

A professor (and likewise his Teaching Assistant) is vulnerable to the extent that he or she is concerned about his students' learning, whether that concern is generated externally by staff, departmental, or career pressures, or internally by personal conscience and a sense of responsibility. Claims of not understanding, lack of clarity, difficult presentation, too much material--all of these by students can be used to manipulate the professor into covering more or less material more generally or thoroughly, or simplifying some material, both in class and on tests. These kinds of maneuvers usually take more than one student, usually requiring the unification of a group of students, and/or TA's, or if the problem is a TA, an attempt by the students individually first, then collectively, and if this is ineffectual, a possible alliance with the professor. Do not expect major revisions in the course, but a nickel and diming away of certain requirements or plans for alternative ones. Most courses have course evaluations at the end and professors know, especially untenured ones, that if enough static is generated by students it may affect their future career security and outlook, though most are more worried about their record as concerns publishing, rather than teaching. If you cannot get satisfaction from a professor during the course, be sure to spell this out in writing and encourage others to do so as well, in your individual anonymous evaluations of him/her at the end of the semester. If the situation is critical, letting him or her know you are going to do this is probably not wise, since the situation is probably galvanized beyond any manipulation, but you may consider it if you can get a group of unified students to approach the professor's superior and voice their concerns--this too may be an impotent act with certain risks akin to approaching an appeals committee, but continued pressure like this cannot be ignored forever, and you may be helping the next class he/she teaches with your actions and acid course evaluations.

Remember, you too, as a defacto member of this hierarchy, are also vulnerable. Obviously, your central vulnerability is in terms of grades, especially when your grade involves a subjective measure by the professor, or TA, such as class participation, or evaluation of your opinion(s) in a writing assignment or essay; or if you have gone over his head to complain or been a vocal questioner and/or critic of his presentation--or ruffled his feathers in even the slightest way. Beyond this, you are vulnerable when you do not meet your responsibilities as a student, such as paper deadlines, reading assignments, or any other area where you appear to be "not working hard enough." More will be said about this in other sections of Special Concerns and Strategies. Good Special Concerns and Strategies Skills will not replace thorough, disciplined study in helping you to achieve the best grades possible, but they can maximize your chances of those grades being congruent with or above your actual ability.

OTHER HIERARCHIES

Of course, there are other hierarchies that I have not mentioned that will affect you at college. Hierarchies involving others, such as employers, roommates, and parents will exist and become apparent, and should be investigated and outlined. This is the first use for your Special Concerns and Strategies Notebook.

Construct and outline all the hierarchies that could have a current, potential affect on you. Besides the ones concerning college courses, become aware of the power relationships between you and your parents or guardian(s), other family members, roommates, and employer(s).

When is a Hierarchy like a Curve?

You will notice that I began by mentioning curves and ended up with illustrating hierarchies. Do not be mislead by the concreteness of my hierarchical drawings, power relationships are much more aptly thought of as the best curve drawn to a group of related points on a graph. Solid lines and even wavy curves are only approximations to simplify what is complex and to help us perceive an overall pattern. What actually exists is often more complex.

Recall the discussion of linear v.s. constellational thinking (p. 34) and indulge the following fictitious parable:

The world's best physics professor of mechanics and the world's best bowler are rolling ten frames against each other. The professor approaches the game with his tape measure and slide rule, and a machine that rolls his bowling ball with exacting spin and force after extensive analysis of the bowling ball in his laboratory. The world's best bowler arrives having had a good night's sleep and a good breakfast.

The first five frames are even with neither of the protagonists able to gain an edge. In the first frame, the world's best bowler was ahead, the physics professor having had trouble getting his machine warmed up and securely placed on the alley, but by the third frame, the machine was working properly and the professor was calculating and adjusting it beautifully, and had achieved a slight lead. In the next two frames, both had performed at the top of their ability for the moment, and the match was even.

The sixth frame was a bad frame for both, the bowling balls and the lane was warming up, making the bowling balls lose friction as they warmed the wax in the lane, causing it to become slightly slippery. In the seventh, the professor recalculated the friction coefficient, and professional bowler compensated with a more forceful roll and more hook on his release, learned from years of experience. At the end of the seventh frame, they were still close, but the professional bowler had a slight lead. By the eighth frame, the wax was still warming, and the professor was recalculating, while the professional bowler eyed the sheen coming off the alley as he approached his roll. At the last second he would make intuitive decisions about just how to roll his bowling ball. The professor could not keep up with the warming and cooling of the wax that affected his recalculation of the friction coefficient and was falling behind, but suddenly he had an idea. Quickly he installed a small temperature probe halfway down the lane, and then two others a fourth and three-fourths of the way down the lane in order to get an average, and in the ninth frame he closed to within a point of the world's best bowler. In the tenth they both rolled a strike and in extra frames too. The contest would be decided by a final roll from each.

The professor went first, his calculations correct. The professional bowler rolled second, deciding at the last second to use the opposite side of the lane that had not been warmed by the travel of the last ten frames. His ball hit with ferocious and deadly accuracy. Both bowlers had rolled strikes. Who won the match?

If you read this story carefully, you know that the world's best bowler won the match by one point because of his ability, culled from experience, to intuitively adjust to the conditions of the alley just by looking over the sheen coming off the waxed, wooden surface of the lane. The professor rolled a fine game, but was not able to adjust to conditions, nor perceive them as quickly nor as accurately as the professional bowler.

The professor's game is like linear thinking, able to measure and hold one limited variable at a time. The professional bowler's game is like constellational thinking because it relied on his ability to integrate many variables wholistically and accurately. The professor knew the temperature and thus the friction conditions at three points in the lane. The professional bowler took account of the whole surface of the lane, as infinite a number of variables in the lane as there are points in a line.

In the context of power curves, hierarchies and human relationships it is not possible to use instruments like rulers and thermometers to measure variables or to integrate them with a calculator or a slide rule; your only instrument will be yourself, to become a kind of human barometer of psychological states, and human interactions. How well you can observe, and gauge the many variables of human behavior and find creative solutions to your problems will greatly determine the outcomes of your inevitable interface with power curves.

EXERCISES: THE POWER CURVE

Understand and accept the extent and limits of the following

concepts: Power Curve

Hierarchy

Pressure Points

Linear v.s. Constellational Thinking

For practice, construct a hierarchy of your family, including

these vital details: Who is a member?

Who has what power and influence?

Who has what responsibilities?

Where are you in this hierarchy?

After doing this determine how responsibilities mesh so that everything that needs to be done gets done, how power entails responsibility, and what pressure points via responsibility or other

SPECIAL CONCERNS AND STRATEGIES
Lesson Two: Reconnaissance and Intelligence

The goal in this exercise is to find and prepare to meet potential enemies and allies. The key to reconnaissance and intelligence is perceptive, trained observation and knowing what you want to do with the information. One must know what one is looking for and how to ascertain it and what the purpose of knowing is, but first one must know where to look.

Consult your outlines of hierarchies, here you will find potential enemies and allies, and your current power relationships with them. Your next task is to complete a dossier on each person, starting with the most powerful and influential person(s) in each hierarchy. Gather the following intelligence on each one wherever applicable and available:

Full name, age, race, position or job, special life experiences, life goals, tenured or untenured, years at university, area(s) of expertise, publications, textbooks written, what part of the country are they from, educational background, where they went to elementary, junior high, high school, college?, salary and/or other means of support, kind of car they drive or would like to drive, kind of house they live in, sexual preference, married or unmarried, committed or solo, status of their important relationships, parents living, where do they live and what is the conditions of their lives, dietary habits, entertainment preferences, personal passions, relationship with wife or husband, or other significant others, number and ages of children, where they go to school, their children's interests and accomplishments, what are their children's goals in life, any and all unsubstantiated scuttlebutt you hear from anyone (try to get it substantiated), your perception of their general attitude toward life, or anything else and how it changes with their mood, whether they are moody, what are their politics, where do they stand on the important political issues, religious preference, level of devotion to religion, attitudes toward love, where they went on vacation last, excesses or limits in any area, personal failures, broken relationships and divorces and their affects, financial condition, financial responsibilities, debts, credit ratings, previous jobs or careers, reputation in the capacity that you will deal with them most, hobbies and outside interests, special talents and capacities in any area, physical condition, limitations, or special abilities etc.-- in short, EVERYTHING AND ANYTHING of possible relevance you can find out about the person.   Note these and any other information in your special notebook for this purpose.

What will you do with this accumulation of information? Each dossier will probably not contain all the aforementioned items, but try to collect enough material so that you have some solid notions about the person your interested in. The purpose here is to size up this person so as to be able to predict their likes, dislikes, and general response patterns--to make them a predictable quantity. Certainly in the academic sphere, much of this kind of information is easily attainable about you, though rarely do professors or TA's delve into it. You should know them at least as well as they can know you, and better if at all possible, because knowing what you are up against, knowing a potential enemy, is basic to any possible

conflict situation. Some of these items are easily available from
the department office the person works in, or from the school
administration, library, phone book, or just by asking a secretary.
Luckily, most people's favorite topic is themselves, especially if
they can brag some or recall a pleasant memory in the process.
Key to your success in intelligence gathering is that the potential
enemy or ally remain unaware that you are probing with intent.
For this you need to know when you can lead with a topic and
when you must wait for their lead. The goal of all of these
techniques is to invite the person you are seeking information
about into one of the most enjoyable and easily carried on human
activities--talking about themselves. You can begin to access
his/her information in the following ways:

INNOCUOUS QUESTIONS

These questions are probing, but expected as part and parcel of
everyday conversation. Just being friendly and a good
conversationalist can get you much information about a person's
present frame of mind, future plans or past experiences. The
questions asked have to be non-threatening, fit in with the
discussion by following the lead of the person you are speaking
with, and not be a frontal attack on something you really would
like to know. For instance, a person says, in the course of
things,"I need a vacation." You can ask,"where would you like to
go?" Time allowing, this might lead into a discourse on why this
person likes whatever place he/she names, with you sharing
vacation places you've been to or would like to go to and why

(which can be fictitious in regards whether you would actually like to go there, but you must know what you are talking about). In this way, you could find out something about this person. If she/he says they want a week in Manhattan, then they are different from someone who want ten days on the Boundary Waters in Minnesota. Other examples:

You see an obvious family portrait on a desk and say,

"Nice picture, is this your family?"

"Is this your family, your daughter looks just like my sister."

"Who did this portrait for you?"

"Nice picture, I always hated poising for those things."

Any of these comments, either in the form of a direct or rhetorical question, can start the person talking about their family, and will get you much more information than looking them in the eye and saying, "Could you tell me about you and your family?"

ASK FOR ADVICE

This technique works especially well when the questioner is young and the respondent is old and considers themselves in possession of some wisdom that they are compelled by age to impart. You can take the lead. Ask something that you know the person knows about. This can be anything from kayaks, to investment decisions, how to study for his/her test, where the best restaurants are for a formal date, what kind of used car to buy-- anything they are bound to know or at least have an opinion on and would enjoy telling you.

GETTING HELP WITH A PROBLEM

This works especially well with someone whose responsibility it is to help you learn, like a TA's or professor, and sometimes employers, if you knowing what you ask helps their business. The problem you have can be fictitious, or it can really be something you do not understand. Perhaps your first visit for this purpose should be genuine, to see what the person is like in this situation, but after this you might want to develop an involved, fictitious problem that you understand (if you come away confused, you've just learned what to expect from this person as a teacher or that something is lacking in your understanding) so you won't have to listen too carefully to the person's explanations and can concentrate on what you will say next to accomplish your real purpose. Use this as a starter for discussion of other issues that are invited by the person or their surroundings. If there is a computer modem or a naked person serving croissants in the room, its probably ok to ask innocuous questions about those things. One can learn about the person as a teacher, and otherwise, using this technique.

ASK ABOUT SOMETHING RELATED TO A CLASS TOPIC-GET THEIR OPINION

The movement of this kind of discussion is from factual about the person's subject area to a political view and why. If you want to get a full load of opinion from someone, ask them these kinds of questions when you are alone with them or as few people as possible are around, and show that you care about the topic, whether you do or not. A chemistry professor has just given a lecture in which he explained the chemical reaction that occurs in the upper atmosphere that causes acid rain. Later, you might ask him/her what they think might be a solution to the problem, and you will probably learn something about their environmental views as well. This same method can be used with almost any topic, from economics, to philosophy to art (never ask a philosophy professor his opinion on anything unless you are prepared to listen intently, and feign enthrallment for what will seem a very long time). Almost every topic of pure knowledge has political connections, and consequences.

The goal of each of these method is to start the person talking freely about themselves. You will undoubtedly mix techniques in any given conversation. Of course, you may run up against someone who really does not feel like talking that day, or is an intensely private person who doesn't share themselves, especially with students. Also be aware that the person may not be telling the truth, though usually a person tells at least a half-truth in the process of trying not to reveal certain truth. Usually, however, even the most vaulted person will launch into a monologue about themselves if they feel comfortable with you, or if they regard you as a stranger or powerless subordinate, without effect in their lives.

WHAT TO EXPECT FROM PROFESSOR

In the academic sphere, professors will often be at the top of your hierarchies, have the most power, and be in a position to do you the most harm. He/She will be one of the first people you seek intelligence information about. College could be a wondrous place if all classes were small, students were unafraid to make mistakes in class, and the teachers/professors actively interacted with their students instead of lecturing ad nauseam. Often there will be several sections of a course taught by different people. This can give you the unique opportunity to evaluate them as teachers and chose a section. You probably won't be able to do this when you register, but sometimes you can drop-add into a better teacher's section, or at least out of a perfectly lousy teacher's section. Look for the following characteristics in a good teacher:

*Initial positive impression

*Question and answer style of lecturing, and encourages class to offer guesses when they are stumped.

*Pays more than lip service to the maxim," there is no such thing as a stupid question," to the extent that he indulges really stupid questioners (up to a certain point, when an after class consultation is offered instead of holding up the rest of the class) and scolds those who scorn them.

*Available and ready at office hours, or by appointment.

*Can speak English that doesn't sound like he just finished an "English As A Second Language" course.

*Can get at the question behind the question from students who cannot quite formulate their question--can get at exactly what it is the student does not understand.

*Sense of Agreeable Pace--speed material is dished out equals speed students can take it in.

*Will work difficult problems or problems outside the scope of the text as examples, will risk the embarrassment of his/her own tentativeness or failure.

*Lectures show more preparation than just thinking about what he/she is about to say during the walk from the office down to the lecture hall.

*Syllabus agrees with what he/she does in class, be wary of disparities, they often show up as test questions that you did not think you had to prepare for because the topic wasn't on the syllabus, and was only talked about for 5-10 minutes.

*Sense of Humor--knows when to seek comic relief with a joke, tells funny jokes, can take a joke, can be the butt of a joke, can let students make jokes.

Of course, all of this may be a far cry from what you can, and likely will get stuck with.

In fact, most professors, to a greater or lesser extent, cultivate a professional distance based on the idea that "familiarity breeds contempt" because they do not want to get into a situation where they might lose their supposed "objectivity," or where they might have to fail someone they like. This "professional distance" can work to your advantage in that the professor will not be scrutinizing you, other that as a series of test grades, and in other areas you can seem to be almost anything and he/she will accept whatever it is on face value, not wanting to look any further. This gives you great latitude in cultivating any enhanced image (described later) of yourself you might choose, and it just makes sense to choose one they will like, enjoy giving high grades to, and be willing to write glowing recommendations about. Never fear that the professor will not get to know you well enough to write a believable recommendation, he/she will want to be perceived as a thoughtful, perceptive, dedicated evaluator and will often cozy up and humanize their depiction of their relationship with you to do so. In actuality, their recommendation will be based on only what they know, your academic performance and the image your give them to cozy up to and humanize.

Why is this so? Because if you gave them yourself, it would threaten their posture of professional distance, and call on them to give more of themselves in return. God (and power relationships) forbid that we should really be honest about our needs and wants and dreams and really get to know each other. We might have to change the way we live, we might get hurt, we might end up looking like a fools, or lose all that we've worked so hard for (that often doesn't really satisfy us anyway), or be accused of indiscretions with a student--the risks are just too great and images and distance are so much easier to manage. Thus is the game played.

Conversely, you may find professors and others who are genuinely willing to share themselves, often when you are an obviously bright student, or a student they meet who does not take classes in their department, and does not poise as much of a risk. You may actually become friends, in some remote sense of that word. As friends, the two of you run the usual risks of friendship, being used, betrayed or rejected, although if you are used in a scandalous way, say for sexual experimentation, the professor runs the risk of public condemnation, and you the stigma of victim, unwilling or otherwise. If you are a student in your friendly professor's class, be very careful of this friendship, for if you have a tiff, your grade may suffer the consequences.

Given the circumstances, it is not to your advantage to try to blaze a new trail and become friends with everyone. Appearing to be friendly is not the same as becoming friends. Hopefully, you will have friends, usually with people who are not in relationships with you where they hold power over you, because it is safer and allowable to discover yourself as you reveal yourself with them; with few or no repercussions if they should become judgmental. For those who have power over the outcomes of your efforts and ultimately your gains in life, let yourself be represented by a well-conceived and comfortably portrayable enhanced image of yourself, an image that you can manipulate and that they can take satisfaction in, based on your reconnaissance of them collectively and as individuals.

SPECIAL CONCERNS AND STRATEGIES
Lesson Three: The Strategy of Image Enhancement

You have completed and continued Basic and Advanced Concerns and Strategies, have accepted, understood and outlined your current, crucial power curves in the form of hierarchies, and have done reconnaissance on members of these hierarchies. Your goal in this present exercise is to understand and begin to use the central strategy, Image Enhancement, available to you.

I have already introduced the concept of and reasons for creating a likeable image. Next comes the task of choosing one you can easily portray, one in which you can "be yourself" to some extent, but do not necessarily have to portray all of yourself. Your deportment must appear as natural as possible, therefore you will do what all smart, and successful Hollywood casting directors do to one extent or another--you will, in effect, typecast yourself in your role as you. This, I assure you, is much easier than it sounds. Consider the following process.

Begin with considering what you are and would like to be--your natural way of being. For discussion purposes I will call this your I AM/CAN BE mode. Your I AM/CAN BE mode contains every behavior, thought pattern, or feeling you naturally manifest (much of your awareness of these should come from Basic Concerns and Strategies, so if you completed and continued it, you should not have too much trouble thinking of "ways of being" that fit this description). You might want to make a list, notating different situations you have been in and your natural way of handling them. Recall situations where your natural way of being gave desirable results. Next, think about situations were your natural way of being caused undesirable results and how you might have chosen a different behavior that could have changed the result to a more favorable, desired one. This second, other mode of being we will call the BUT I SHOULD HAVE BEEN/BUT I WILL BE mode. Choose behaviors for the BUT I WILL BE mode only from the I AM/CAN BE mode. The completed formulation is as follows:

I AM/CAN BE ???, BUT I WILL BE ???, based on my reconnaissance and daily observation of ???? (person, situation, other), because ???? (person, situation, other) controls ?? (something important to my existence, goals, objective in personal growth, well-being, other). I will be in my BUT I WILL BE mode, created from my I AM/CAN BE mode, tailored so that this ???? (person, situation, other) might best appreciate me--so as to have a desirable result in my interactions with ???? (person, situation, other that controls something important to you).

This simple description encompasses the complex process of Image Enhancement. Your task in creating and portraying an enhanced image is not to create a new, other self; but to select and amplify aspects and possibilities of yourself to the end of creating a favorable impact on whoever this selective creation will best appease or impress. Ask yourself what this person would expect and like or how you could be much like those he/she loves. Incumbent in all this is that you not show aspects of yourself that this person might find disagreeable. You will use the image you create for each person to assert some control over their collective impression of you without doing them any undue psychological harm while perhaps protecting yourself from possible injury.

For instance, you assess a professor who has absolute power over your final grade as being definitively pro-family. You know yourself to be somewhat pro-family, but also pro-choice as regards divorce and abortion. As you interact with this professor about the academic topics, casually throw in a word or two about your family; humorous resolution of conflict with parents or siblings, family reunion stories, how you want to raise your children slightly different from how you were raised if you think he/she will look favorably on your modifications--become a regular Readers Digest of family virtue and piety, and do not broach topics like birth control, divorce, or abortion unless you are sure you can bring forth an agreeable weave of the topic into the discussion for the professor's inspection and near certain approval. If asked directly, fudge your viewpoint enough so that it is nearly indistinguishable from his or hers, or say that you do not know and have not decided yet. This requires discretion--and discretion really is the better part of valor when presenting controversial opinions in an academic setting and is essential in conveying a likeable image.

Note that this is an interactive process, and thus will require daily effort and attention. From your reconnaissance you will only be able to attain a general assessment of a person. It will be prudent of you to verify this assessment by your daily observation, besides using this opportunity and aforementioned techniques to gain further valuable intelligence. As your interactions and observations of this person accumulate, you will make daily changes in your image portrayal so that you accomplish your

promotions, and other opportunities, are bestowed. Thus your perceived performance and image, accurate or not, in the academic world or otherwise, will determine to some greater degree your ability to provide yourself with the means you may need for your personal growth.   Although not necessarily one in the same, your perceived performance and image versus your personal growth-your real objective-are irrevocable linked. Without the means to pursue your real interests, or interest outside the workplace, your personal growth will be hindered. (Where would Michael Jordan be without money for tennis shoes, where would Galileo be without money for a telescope, where would you be without money or a loan for your college education?) It is one thing to have the ability, it is quite another to have the means. Ironically, if we as a society provided those with the ability the means necessary--there would be little need for the distinctions or methods I prescribe in this book. Until this happens, if ever, try to strike a balance between generating enough of the right performance and correct image necessary to maintain means sufficient enough to seek your real objective(s)--your continuing to become and be the person you want to be. Remember, in your practice of Image Enhancement, your purpose is not to harm others, but to avoid harm: an enhanced image used for any other reason besides personal self-defense is without purpose other than to deceive others for one's own personal gain--at their expense.   It, as well as outright fraudulent representation, will be used against you by many you may happen to encounter. Be aware of your own potential for these capacities, as well as that of those multitudes with whom you share that campus--and this planet.

IMAGE ENHANCEMENT EXERCISES

To practice reconnaissance and intelligence and the uses of image creation and portrayal:

Part One

Pretend you are a celebrity and famous for something and a guest on your favorite television talk show. Imagine what questions the host would ask you and how you would respond in order to maintain your celebrity image.

Part Two

1) Compile a dossier on yourself.

2) Imagine a I AM/CAN BE mode.

3) Build an image, via imagining an BUT I WILL BE mode, from yourself that you would like.

4) Act out or imagine acting out the image you create and see if you like it via your dossier.

This part of the exercise may be a difficult mind game for you, but I am hopeful that you will at least attempt it. If you do this and find it easy, you probably did not indulge the exercise with much depth and thought, though there are always exceptions. If you found it difficult to maintain perspective as to which person you were, the image or yourself for yourself (difficulty in separating the I AM/CAN BE mode from the BUT I WILL BE mode), while liking yourself all through, you now have at least an inkling of the difference between being an enhanced image of yourself, and just being yourself. Your difficulty indicates a good grasp of Basic Concerns and Strategies and an integrated self. If you did this and created an image that at some level you did not like, investigate and try to find out why, and review Basic Concerns and Strategies. If you have a very negative reaction to this process, you may want to consider seeking professional psychological, or psychiatric help.

Part Three

1) Compile a dossier on someone you have had difficult dealings with in the past (or are having difficulty with at present, if the situation between the two of you is not too polarized).

2) Take the I AM/CAN BE mode you imagined in Part One, and use it to create an image via the BUT I WILL BE mode (sometimes it is helpful for some people to also imagine a "but I won't be" mode, though the transition to actually portraying the image can be more difficult if you are trying to not do versus just trying to do). Compare the image you propose with the dossier you made to see if there are any glaring incongruences.

3) Imagine being the image you have created with the person from the past that you had difficulty with, or if you are confident and brave, try first imagining, then portraying the image for the

present person with whom you are having difficulty. Imagine possible situations and how you might instantaneously adjust your enhanced image.

4) Evaluate. Would this work for you? Could you do it? Would or did this work better for you than what you were doing? Can you continue to do it?

In all of this it is most important to remember Rule Number One of SPECIAL CONCERNS AND STRATEGIES--TO NEVER SACRIFICE YOUR SENSE OF SELF. Maintain it, baby it, never jeopardize it. Do not let anything threaten it, including the instructions in this book. Without it initially and continuously reviewed and known, and kept as a safe, secure haven from which to indulge exospection, the effective use of Special Concerns and Strategies will be severely limited. Notice that Parts One and Two of these exercises are purely introspective, all tasks take place in the relative calm of the individual and spiritual self, first introduced and defined in Advanced Concerns and Strategies. Part Three begins an interface between one's introspective calm and the turbulent exospective tasks that involve career decisions and interactions with others. As you become more experienced in dealing with this interface in meeting the demands of life, you may find that, as regards your career, you can share your individual, unadulterated self in satisfying ways, but you may not be able to always share this self with all people you meet. You will develop a sense for knowing who the trustworthy people are. You won't feel that they are out to get you, even if they could. You will trust them (to some degree). Many will probably fall into the category of friends or lovers, but some may be passing strangers, neighbors, co-workers and on occasion, colleagues. Enjoy them where you find them, for in my experience they are somewhat rare. When you think you've found one, open up yourself slowly, test the waters, if your trust is well-founded, the possibilities of this trust being honored and respected will still be there tomorrow. Conversely, do not let these kinds of opportunities pass you by. Being just an enhanced image of yourself always and forever may be a worse fate than the consequences of not being so in certain situations.

SPECIAL CONCERNS AND STRATEGIES
Lesson Four: Day to Day Confrontations -- Your Arsenal

This is where you make or break the opportunities that will be given you. Daily observation and adjustments will be required. You will have your hands full.

You have several methods at your disposal to help you complete your portrayal of a self image that you should already be considering, but first a few additional points about image selection. Keep in mind that you do not want to stray too far from your natural self, you just want to be selective and reserved about what you present. In this way, you can continue to maintain an authenticity and genuineness that is hard to feign. Also, keep in mind that you do not have to present the same selected image to each person, but can vary your presentation per each individual. Only in cases where two people you meet may interact and compare notes on you do you have to be cognizant of keeping a coherent presentation between them. This can happen between two or more fellow students, or two TA's or professors who are team teaching, or in a social situation where you are talking to a group. You will learn how to keep it light and bright in these kinds of situations, but be cautious, for the possibility does exist that you could get caught manifesting diverse, and in the eyes of some, contradictory opinions and behaviors. Fortunately, situations with the necessary depth for this to happen are rarely encountered, though if you are confused or unsure about what selective image to portray, there is an appropriate strategy to employ. Inconspicuousness is the historical choice.

Becoming inconspicuous in word and deed, and if possible appearance is a good strategy to employ under the aforementioned circumstances. This is also a good first days strategy, giving you the time to do the complete, necessary reconnaissance required to formulate image selection and portrayal. In the holocaust of World War Two, Jews and others in the camps who survived often did so by becoming inconspicuous--blending in with the surroundings and their fellow prisoners so well, that the brutal Nazi authorities took no notice of them, allowing them to get along without incident, clinging to life until the camps were liberated. You can use this method too, but the stakes will not be nearly as high, nor the measures necessary so drastic. Simply blend in to the background of whatever situation you are in; become a part of the thousands of students that this person has seen and is seeing, wear the usual campus uniform, blue jeans and a T-shirt. Ask the usual questions, say the usual things, make the usual mistakes. Do not make an impression, if possible. Silent motionlessness is best in lecture hall. Don't even nod, unless you cannot help yourself, or the lecturer makes eye contact with you. Avoid this by not sitting in the front. Bide your time, make your observations and calculations, there will be plenty of time to make an impression later, and when you do you will know more about what you are trying to do, and will make the correct and best one possible via your selected image. Do nothing with flair, just do it if asked. Remain a blank page that the person observing you will fill in with standard, unremarkable, status quo student type conclusions.

You cannot maintain this posture indefinitely however, nor should you, for it is to your advantage to make a favorable impression that will win you personal kudos from those in power. Synthesize and portray your selective image using the following methods.

APPEARANCE

Become your most agreeable, attractive self--based entirely on their standards. Consider the possibility of "dressing for success," or getting your "colors" analyzed--remember you can always do this yourself. Ask yourself--what would this person like or find acceptable? At college, jeans and cotton mesh shirts are ok in general, but if you are in the business school, the atmosphere may demand a more refined wardrobe, like pinpoint oxfords and slacks. You can say things about yourself with your dress, but be sure not to say the wrong things. Saying, with clothes, "I'm capable and attractive" is different from saying, "I capable and an absolute knockout, more sexy and attractive than any man/woman on this campus" or "I'm the most competent, intelligent, creative and capable person here, and I'm damn attractive too." Do not understate or overstate yourself via you choice of wardrobe, but if you are Ms. America or Einstein, be that person on the inside, while tempering your outward appearance. People, including TA's and professors can be jealous of your good looks or brilliant abilities. Save the former for friends and lovers, and the latter for tests or papers. Use and groom your appearance to create the right image to make that favorable impression that will help you get what you want, whether that be a good grade or coveted job offer.

For some, dressing well will not be an affordable option. Do the best you can. Wear clean clothes, even if they are old, take care of yourself, have a healthy glow about you. You will have to work somewhat harder in other areas to make up for this shortfall, but sometimes poverty managed correctly can also make a good impression. After all, many of those at the top where not always at the top, though some, once there, may have forgotten this. Hopefully, those of you who are poor, but bright will be fortunate enough to meet and be supervised by those who were also once poor and bright, and some identification will occur, in that you will remind them of themselves and become part of their admiration for their own grit. If you see this kind of identification happening, nurture it, and let it work to your advantage.

POLITENESS AND MANNERS

As hollow as this is, it has carried some people who are lacking in every other category a long way. You've heard it before, "He's not handsome, but he's nice" or " She's not real smart, but she's so nice." In fact, you can do some incredibly nasty things to people while being nice and if nobody looks any further, you could come out looking like a million and smelling like a rose, and still have successfully destroyed someone. What is "being nice" anyway?

It starts with getting into the vernacular of the setting you are in. Yes and no ma'am may be alright in the Southern U.S., but up North could be considered too patronizing. In general, please and thank you are universally accepted and expected. A large part of this is how you say it, and what you look like to the person when you said it. An impatient, sarcastic "Thank You" won't get you many brownie points. Note how these people treat each other when they seem to be treating each other nicely and simply take the time to pleasantly imitate them, even if you'd really like to rip their vocal cords out so they couldn't say,"It will be just a few more minutes" again. Surprisingly, you can show your frustration with a long wait, or anything else disagreeable and attempt to change it in the process--and still be nice! For instance, instead of saying," Jesus Christ, this is taking a helluva long time, can't you do something!?" you might say, "You must be terribly busy today, maybe I could come back at a more convenient time." The first is probably stated loudly, standing bold upright, the latter, perhaps stooped down close to whomever you are speaking to, and said in a wee voice. Either will get you a response, but its my bet that the latter will get you the more agreeable, helpful response. And... you will also make a favorable impression.

These same arguments can be extended to social situations. When in Rome, do as the Romans do, even if the pretentiousness of the situation calls forth all your fortitude not to burst out laughing. Hold that cup correctly, use that silverware in the correct order, eat and comment on things in the proper way and order if you perceive one to be in force. If you blunder, simply apologize to whomever you may have offended, and correct the behavior. Do not throw their stupidity back at them, no matter how much the situation may call for it, for their stupidity is often only an extension or symptom of a more serious inequity or problem; instead try to directly affect that problem in another way by talking to members of the party alone, after the party. Do not spoil the party for anyone, or risk your image, or theirs. Air disaffections in groups of not more than you and one other, if at all, and realize the possible risks in airing unpopular perceptions to your cultivated enhanced image.   Ask yourself, is this person worth trusting, worth being my real self with, and worthy of my confidence? Do I have to worry about damaging any favorable impression I have gained if I do this?

NON-AGGRESSIVE BEHAVIOR
AND OMNISCIENT AWARENESS

This requires perceptive, daily observation and the ability to hid anger and resentment until a more appropriate time comes to release it. Observe those you interact with daily, note how they seem to be feeling. Realize there will be day to day differences in how someone is, and that you will have to adjust your enhanced image accordingly. I cannot emphasize the timely aspect of this point enough, for what was a reasonable human being on Monday can become a tyrannical master by Friday. The causes of this can be multifold, but the important thing is that your perceive the current human condition of your potential, evershifting enemies and allies. They can change, and consequently, you can change in response; to nullify or cushion the negative situations that they may throw you into. Listen to how they talk. The sound of their voice may tell you how they are feeling. Watch how they move and note their energy level. Are they enthusiastic, listless, or exhausted? If they are angry, especially if they are pedagogues under someone's thumb, they may take it out on you if you give them half a chance, and even if you don't. From early mannerisms, try to gain an insight into how they are feeling that day and adjust you interaction with them accordingly--is it a kid gloves kind of day, or can you speak forth with some force of conviction, sure that it will be taken as dedication to the pursuit and understanding of topic rather than as a personal affront?

Why is this especially important in classroom situations? Because your only representation of achievement and effort in these encounters is the grade you receive, and your non-graded interactions may greatly influence the actual grade you get or your bargaining position in the future if you get into grade-related trouble. The solution to these kinds of problems is so simply that it is often overlooked. The solution is preventative-get liked, be agreeable, even if you are not. Be pleasant, even though you're the baddest, nastiest, most self-seeking human mother----er to cross the instructor's path since last year's class. Even if you are Mother Theresa incarnate, you still may have to temper yourself and choose an image to get liked, since nobody will be able to believe you are so others-orientated. Even if the instructor does not like you, be nice to him/her. Kill 'em with kindness, but do not overdo it by fawning too much. Never give false praise, but occasionally give select praise that can actually be seen as deserved. Always be courteous and considerate, especially involving punctuality and use of their time.   Never purposefully antagonize the instructor and risk making him/her angry or upset at you, neither for truth or honor, for truths (about power relationships) beyond the one you are pursuing will become all too evident if you proceed, and the truth you are seeking, if it really is there, will be there no matter what the result of your joust, and while the honor of making your point by defeating the instructor publicly may be a sweet victory, it can only be coveted temporarily, and may inflict a personal cost to you that was not worth the prize.   I am not suggesting that not pressing a point is always the action one should take, but invariably in your dealings with pedagogues you will realize there are limits in each individual case.   Respect these limits or understand and prepare for the possible consequence if you overstep them.   In my experience, there are situations where standing your ground and risking interpersonal conflict and future difficulties are worthy endeavors because of the gravity and importance of the issue at hand, but usually this in not the case in classroom dealings with pedagogues.   Keep all of this in mind before you willingly step on their professional toes.

CREATING PSYCHOLOGICAL INDENTUREMENT

This is an advanced capacity. If you are able to perceive the opportunities and take advantage of them in a timely fashion you probably will have mastered most of the possibilities of image enhancement. Unfortunately, you cannot take the initiative and cause conditions to make psychological indenturement possible. They can only happen if the person you are interested in indenturing makes a blunder or asks you to do something above and beyond what normally would be expected. Often, it is hard to tell if one has actually achieve this, until the situations changes and you are treated in a more favorable way than you expected--and you seem to know why. Something you did or did not do that not everyone would be incline to do with the definiteness, grace and consideration that you exhibited spontaneously, without direction-- these are the kind of occurrences that set you apart and may achieve Psychological Indenturement.

The possible scenarios for this to happen are quite simple. A person in near absolute power over you for the moment says an unkind, disrespectful word directed at you, in front of others, which you probably do not deserve and do not respond to in kind. Instead, you say nothing and let the silence of others work on their conscience, or you say something disarming, or in some sense turn away the insult in an understanding way while maintaining your dignity. If this person shows any remorse for doing this, either in the form of an apology or their manner towards you, and you are still kind and understanding about everything--you now have this person indentured to you. You were kind to them when you had every reason to be otherwise, and they have realized this, and feel bad about what they have done. You can be sure that they will now treat you with a little more consideration than others who have not shown them this kindness.

Another example is when someone with near absolute power over you for the moment is in need and in a bind, and you do something for them that gets them out of the bind and on their way, something that you did not have to do for them---then you have achieve this same favored status. They owe you one. If they have a conscience, they will see this and try to think of something to even the score, or return the favor, depending on their view of giving and receiving. Remarkably, the less you remind them of it, the more likely you are to reap its greater rewards.

The key to this is the person's own reaction to what they have done or needed. If they can pass off their behavior as justified or are the kind of person who does not feel this kind of contrition, then they will not become indentured no matter what the sin, though it is my personal belief that these people deserve your consideration even more than those who are likely to be repentant, who knows, they may change, and your behavior might be the agent for them changing and learning. The reason that getting someone psychological indentured is an advanced capacity is that it takes more than just being appropriately dressed, polite, aware, and acting non-aggressively: it takes genuine understanding and insight into another person's character, and a large measure of involvement and security in one's own.

This completes SPECIAL CONCERNS AND STRATEGIES. Hopefully you have understood the concepts presented here and this understanding will be productive. The theory and intent of these explanations has been to better prepare you for the realities of academic life, where many things that you did not expect can and will happen. Using these techniques and methods it is my contention and hope that you will have more allies than enemies by avoiding the conditions that generate enemies, and will deal with the enemies you undoubtedly will have more effectively and to your best advantage.

SPECIAL CONCERNS AND STRATEGIES
Summary of Usage

Prepare to recognize, meet and deal effectively with potential enemies and allies by:

1) Noting the Rules of Special Concerns and Strategies.

*Never sacrifice sense of self.

*Accept and understand power relationships.

*Accept the sole objective of striving to achieve the best grades possible.

*Do what is necessary to fulfill the penultimate rule   (Rule No. 3).

2) Begin a special notebook for this purpose, separate from journal suggested for Basic/Advanced Concerns and Strategies, containing reflections on the following (this list is progressive and cumulative):

A) Note the existence of all hierarchies you are a member of and include these details:

*Who is a member?

*Who has what power and influence?

*Who has what responsibilities?

*Where you are in this hierarchy.

Consider possible pressure points and imagine scenarios where they might be needed and the results of their usage.

B) Do reconnaissance and collect all available, applicable, and appropriate intelligence and construct a separate dossier on those in each hierarchy, beginning with those individuals possessing the most influence and power. Use the following methods and sources:

Sources	Methods
Administration	Innocuous questions
Faculty Directory	Ask for Advice
Departmental Office	Help with a Problem
Library	Question related to class
Phone Book	Mixing Techniques
Others you think of?	Others You Think of?

C) Strategy of Image Enhancement:

   *List or imagine"I am/can be" column.

   *Begin to create "But I will be" column from each ongoing dossier you prepared in Step B.

   *Imagine using this image, rehearse in your mind how you will portray it.

   *Do daily and instantaneous updating and re-evaluation of each dossier and image conception/portrayal.

D) Refine and develop your Image Enhancement in regards these finer points and possibilities:

                Appearance

                Politeness and Manners

Omniscient Awareness

Non-Aggressive Behavior

Psychological Indenturement

SPECIAL CONCERNS AND STRATEGIES
Simple Example of Usage

You are hired part-time at a fast food restaurant. The manager is Al Smith, and he is the ultimate authority on site, and though there are shift supervisors, they all take their cues and check every decision with Al. First you do recon on Al. Initially, you find he's in his early thirties, conservative, Republican, white, slightly overweight, lives in a $500 apartment, likes sports, especially baseball, is easygoing until someone screws up, then he gets tense, is willing to help employees when business is hoppin', has a girlfriend named Nan who is very religious, they attend church every Sunday, they are Methodists and serious about each other. He drives a 1985 Chrysler LeBaron, and does not have much contact with employees off the job.

Next, you imagine your I AM/CAN BE mode for this situation: You can be lazy, insightful, creative, reliable, polite, courteous, funny, boisterous, industrious, boring, happy, glowing, vacant, irresponsible etc. Based on your perception of Al and the requirements of the job, you create the BUT I WILL BE mode, deciding to be: polite, courteous, industrious, and reliable. All the rest are not require by Al or the job. You might bone up on baseball scores, find out how his favorite team is doing, and if you are Methodist or practicing another similar religion you might let him know you would like to attend your services on Sunday or at an alternative time, if it would not cause too much trouble with scheduling. Doing these things should place you in his good graces, and help you keep the job, if not also advance. Showing anymore than these traits, unless you sense that they will be appreciated, could be unfortunate. A sense of humor does not serve hamburgers, and might not be appreciated by Al or customers--keep your sense of humor, but keep it to yourself, even sharing it with co-workers may get you in trouble. If you find this and other capacities longing to be use, you may want to look for another job where you can use them or at least express these parts of yourself at little or no risk. Clothes are not an issue here because you are required to wear a uniform, but neatness and cleanliness is, keep yourself neat and clean and presentable. Be aware of the scuttlebutt and gossip going around, but do not try to add to it or become a subject of it by revealing too much of yourself, or stating controversial opinions. You may be able to psychological indenture Al to you by picking up problems at work and dealing with them effectively, before they get out of hand-so that he notices the problem and your solution-and by occasionally working that odd shift that he cannot find anyone for and asks you to fill. Since you were not doing anything then anyway you consent, but do not let Al know this, make it appear that you are making some sacrifice. This may get you forgiveness if you blunder, or favored shift status in the future, or a good recommendation for another, future job. If Al does not seem appreciative, attempt psychological

BETWEEN GAMESMANSHIP AND REAL LIFE:
When To Be Yourself

Nobody can go through life being only an enhanced image all of the time, though some people may try. If I have succeeded in making you aware of how much you really do not want to be adjusting your image, how nice you are and how much you like you just as yourself, then I have accomplished more than I had hoped for. Eventually, sometimes against your will, you will reveal yourself. Hopefully, these revelations will not be at critical times, when you are using a certain image to protect and further your interests, or to control a situation with a potential or actual enemy.

Somehow, thru a process not yet understood (by me), if you meet enough people and cultivate enough images, you will find people who you are comfortable dropping all image enhancement around, and begin to spontaneously show all those traits in your I AM/CAN BE mode. I suggest you do this selectively and in stages. Gradually reveal yourself, carefully testing the waters of trust and mutual honesty. Often you will be disappointed, someone may not have it in them to trust you, someone may not know themselves well enough yet to share themselves, or feel that revealing themselves to you might threaten them or some other relationship they depend on; whatever the reason, you cannot force someone to get close to you, and you really would not want to anyway. The beginnings and continuings of a friendship, being yourself with someone, and this being reciprocated, is beautiful, worthwhile, and priceless, though a relatively rare experience, and can and most likely will happen to you, to some degree, in this life.

Most often the kinds of people who become our friends are somewhat like us; they are at or near our own intellectual level, personal awareness level, and often our socioeconomic level. They may even look like us physically in some ways. In general, if they are in hierarchies with us, they are at or near our level in the hierarchy because of the threat that power relationships poise to our mutual trust. It is rare for there to be a distinct imbalance of power between us and our friends, though people being what they will, this does happen. Most are not in a hierarchy with us, and many are developed before our awareness of hierarchies, power curves, and the like---often in childhood, when blessed ignorance of these things allows us to be our spontaneous, open, unadulterated selves almost all of the time.

When you find someone you can share, and be open and yourself with-a friend-he or she is a rare treasure. This person does what he/she says they will do, does not judge you, but listens to you, and supports you in a way you find comforting and desirable. Where one finds such people I do not know, though I can say that I have been lucky enough to chance on a few.

Some people say," to have friends, be a friend," and," if you have money, you got friends." There is some wisdom in both of these sayings, being friendly and trustworthy certainly may open the door to friendship; and having money to do things together, and not be a burden on another certainly can help, but I believe the roots of friendship go deeper than this--I think it has something to do with the unique personality each person in the friendship is, and the freedom and joy they each feel in having someone so wonderful and understanding to share themselves with, for a time. Unfortunately, friendships do not last forever, we move to new towns with our parents, go to new schools, take new jobs in cities thousands of miles away, or get married, or develop other "significant others" that take us away from our established friends-- and it is then that we truly understand what that person we thought of as friend really meant and means to us because we may feel the void they left when we or they move away. We miss them, and hope there will be others, and there will if we can just be patient enough, and even if no more appear as special as the ones we've known before, we always have our memories of them, and usually an occasional phone call or letter comes our way to remind us of our times together. It is then, after the experience has aged, that we realize how precious our time with them really was, for often our sharing with them was an essential part of our process of coming to know and appreciate ourselves. This experience of friendship leaves us changed somehow, as if we grasp a little more about ourselves and about life. Except in Basic Concerns and Strategies where I hope you might find some suggestions that may help you come to a fuller sense of yourself and what it is to be you, I cannot provide you with any prescription for the experience of friendship, for in finding and having friends you and they are more on your own than in any other experience, delving into the new, often uncharted, unexplored, wondrous territory of each other.

LOVERS

Perhaps the best lovers are best friends first. Or old friends. Friends, nevertheless. The difference, at least in this context, is that with lovers there is a sexual sharing of self, i.e., you each give and receive affection expressed sexually. This author is a near hopeless romantic, but as a strategist I am certain of a few things about love and lovers. First, they take time away from other things; besides time together, one's every thought and effort at sustained concentration can become susceptible to sabotage by continuous emotional barrages of joy, and doubt, and hope, and pure, crazy happiness. When trying to study or accomplish some other important task, these often enjoyable intrusions can be, at least, distracting, and, at worst, disruptive or even destructive (But personally, I wouldn't miss them for the world).

Second, love can make one unreasonable in general, I personally do not think as clearly and logically when in love, especially in the beginning and sometimes well into the affair, though with directed attention it is my contention that I can compensate for this. Your thinking too, may be impaired.

Third, I begin to look at the love as all-important, as if it and three square meals a day could satisfy all my needs (perhaps they could....). One can become lackadaisical concerning the rest of the world, cultivating the attitude "I've got mine and I don't care..." Carefree becomes careless and eventually discriminatorily uncaring.

All together, there are any number of pitfalls unique to each love, but one final universal is that love, almost invariably, causes one to hurt and to suffer. "To love is to suffer" someone once said, and as a young man I did not know and would not have heeded this warning if I had heard it; and suffering can take many forms and my loves brought me suffering, but suffering begat wisdom and knowledge for which I am forever grateful, though late at night, alone, I sometimes wish I still had only the beloved. So, decide carefully about matters concerning love, perhaps you will be fortunate enough to find that one special lover you can love and be loved by for lifetime, or for at least a very long time, and know that love TAKES TIME and you may get hurt, and that surely you will be changed in some significant way by the experience. Temper actions with discretion, good judgement and a balanced approach to life overall, and if love comes your way--don't miss it for the world. (A precautionary note: AIDS, Herpes Simplex Two, Chlamydia, Syphilis, Gonorrhea etc.--need I say more?)

I hope by now you can begin to see the difference between creating and being an image from yourself to control a potential threatening person or situation; and being yourself. The central contrast is between being contrived and censored versus being spontaneous and open. What would happen in daily commerce if we all said exactly what we were thinking all of the time? The results might be an social activist's dream, but the conflicts generated might tear society asunder. Why must we behave in this multi-tiered fashion? Ask any nuclear arms negotiator. It is the nature of competition, all may want peace, but as long as there is a real or imagined threat between countries, or on a lesser scale, between persons, lasting peace and tranquility are not possible.

Competition as a fact of life has changed from a primitive product of our aggressive instinct which enabled us to survive individually and as a species, to modern day blessing and nemesis. In the constitutional United States, by providing the freedom of mind and spirit to generate new ideas, the capitalist free enterprise economic system fosters creativity with the promise of monetary reward beyond the simple pleasure of having achieve one's goal of inventing or discovering a new, better way of doing things. This economic system allowed those with ideas, and a commitment to the hard work necessary to make those ideas a reality, to have a chance to rise to the top and be appropriately compensated for the value of their efforts. Many of us in the United States have benefited economically because of our freedom and the freedom of others to compete and create. Other countries have other systems, but in today's world there is a trend toward allowing those in charge and at risk to directly reap the rewards or consequences of that which they have sown, no matter what system of government they may live under. Our economic enterprises, at least in the developed countries, have evolved well beyond fighting daily to attain basic survival, and our respect for the sanctity of human life has deepened over the centuries so that, consequently, our competitive drive has found new, less life-threatening avenues of expression, via athletic and economic competition that do not necessarily maim and kill. Today's battles are more often fought with words as weapons, all being directed at compelling hearts and minds to embrace different products, or different religious and political ideologies.

Warfare, the natural end result of aggression and intense competition for limited resources necessary to life, is perhaps the only remaining expression of human aggression that has become more deadly and life-threatening; and in a nuclear age it has become our ever-threatening nemesis even though most conflicts are not generated solely by a lack of resources necessary for life, but also include violent disagreement over political and religious ideology. The sword of old, though brutal, savage, and deadly, killed only one at a time, with great risk to the swordsman if involved in combat with an equally armed opponent. The same was true of early firearms, though the luxury of distance and cover from the intended target greatly reduced the risk of personal injury via retaliation. The advent of rapidly repeating machine guns, and bombs thrown by hand, strategically placed in water or on land, or dropped from airplanes greatly increased the damage that one person or a few persons could do, suddenly only one or a few could kill many or a great many. This kill ratio was greatly enhanced by the invention of the atomic bomb, and has been further enhanced by refinements of this original, infamous instrument of war. In the coming of the atomic age and the maintenance of "nuclear readiness," it is for the first time possible to clearly see the potentially devastating results and high costs of our aggressive instinct unleashed. An instinct that made us viable might also make us extinct.

Part of my impetus for writing this book was a by-product of competition--to find a reasonable way of coping with its demands without necessarily adding fuel to its fire. The personal conflict that a preponderance of competitive situations create for individuals can be summarized for each person, and myself, in a single sentence: Competition demands that I often be other than I would like to be so that I may survive and prosper. The conflict between being oneself and the need to compete to survive and prosper is a conflict I believe we all share. Part of this conflict involves having material goods (to have), versus being oneself (to be), but another part is purely psychological, involving how we see ourselves through the eyes of a society-at-large in terms of meeting its expectations for achievement, associated prestige, and attaining the status quo versus how we see ourselves, alone in the dark, on a beach, after watching a beautiful sunset. If we compete to the extent and extreme that we ignore ourselves and what we each like, we may gain much in terms of material wealth, and grow large in the eyes of society, and ourselves if we see ourselves through its eyes, but we may lose the time required to be ourselves, our individual reference point in this life, and become a warriors with no joy and no purpose. Conversely, if we each remain absolutely true to ourselves, our beliefs may hinder us from doing what we need to do to compete, and thus survive, and attain a scale of living that nurtures us, and allows us to prosper as a biological, psychological self. For each individual, if the conflict between needing to compete and one's sense of self is drastic enough, one could cease to exist on some psychological plane, in some terminal way.

The adaptations we each make to changing competitive conditions are like a tug of war between what we each are and would like to be; and what we each need to be to survive and prosper-this synthesis reaching its conclusion in what we each seem to be. If certain aspects of human competition were either modified or eliminated, then there would be greater freedom to be ourselves, what we each are and would like to be, because the current demands that we each need to meet to survive and prosper would be changed or absent, and what we each seem to be would become a closer facsimile of what we each would like to be and are.

There is historical precedent for the expression of our aggressive instinct via our competitive drive changing and becoming more humane, though this change cannot be measured with great strides, but only in tiny steps. No longer do roman gladiators die in the arena, slavery has been abolished, debtor's prisons and workhouses no longer exist, and child labor laws prohibit the exploitation of children, though torture still exists and exploitation via rank and social class, though dulled somewhat by social programs and the welfare state in developed countries, still forces people into unsavory roles. Both the tireless responsibility of supervisory monitoring, and the belittling prospect of fledgling servitude, with the subtle slavery these continuing roles impose on all, from top to bottom, have begun to be questioned. The evolving expression of the human competitive drive has historically been modified by greater consideration for the sanctity of human life, first only for biological life, simple living or dying, but later and lately for our collective psychological life--whether we are happy as people and satisfied as a species. One begins to wonder, in a world where providing nearly everyone with a

EXPERIENCES: Some Realities of Academic Life

The concerns and strategies I have previously outlined came out of many experiences, some where I applied what I have written and others where I learned I should have applied it. Here are several descriptive narratives and the morals derived (all names used are fictitious):

Beginnings

At summer orientation, I visited my future college dormitory for the first time. The place was being renovated and I entered the building by walking up a narrow board placed through an open window. I was wearing blue jeans cutoffs and a tee shirt. The front desk personnel were mingling with the construction workers, someone offered me a beer and I took it just to be social. Six or seven orientees were scheduled to receive a tour of the dormitory, but I was the first to arrive. By the time the others came I was on a first name basis with three construction workers and two gay men who were the front desk personnel, and all of us were very relaxed. The new arrivals were wearing summer casuals, like canvas shorts and cotton mesh shirts and seemed a little tense by comparison. All of us orientees were then ushered into the dormitory director's office, myself still toting half a can of beer. Needless to say, I was an incredible contrast in style to my counterparts, and this first impression went a long way towards the director casting an especially watchful eye in my direction in the year that followed, and none of this group of orientees became friends or even acquaintances of mine, though I did get along well with the two gay men at the front desk, which proved to have some advantages in terms of getting things I needed, like meal tickets, during my stay in the dormitory.

Moral: Fit in or enjoy the consequences. These people reacted to an image of me--an all important first impression, which had very little to do with anything substantive about me. This particular incongruence did not cost me anything in the future, but it was a learning experience.

The Dorm

The first few days living in the dormitory were exciting, but the conversation was tremendously dull and superficial. What's your name, where ya from, what are going to be--these topics, along with the where ises and how toos of any initial experience, dominated discussion and I soon realized that few, including myself, were equipped to answer anymore that the first two questions, and that the real unasked question in everyone's mind was: "What do you think of me?" Soon thereafter I began giving different names, places of former residence and career aspirations to each new person I met. It was great fun as long as I could remember who I told what. After awhile it got too confusing, and situations were evolving where I'd be talking to two people at the same time who I'd given conflicting information to, so I'd come clean, giving my real name, former residence and say I didn't have the foggiest notion what I wanted to be, that I just wanted to live in the present and get to know a few people--in most cases I was greeted with a knowing laugh, in others with mild scorn or a do-

and-say-anything-you-want-it-makes-no-difference-to-me attitude. In a short time, most "forgave" me and I got to know a few people.

Moral: My first unplanned experiment with image management. How easily people accepted what they wanted to hear without probing any further. With some, I'd have been better off not telling them the truth, they would have been more comfortable with me, however, the roles we play may make the day, pave our way, and someday pay, but can (and will) leave use feeling lonely. Even when I "came clean" I did not reveal much about myself except that I was interested in getting to know people and that I didn't know what I wanted to be, and that I had a sense of humor or was a bit of a prankster, depending on your point of view. This sense of honesty endeared me to some and caused me to be held in contempt by others whose roleplaying my behavior challenged. I could have just as easily gotten along better with those I irritated and saved myself their scorn, while still finding those others who I could be less image-conscious around, though I wonder if the sweet communions with the latter would have been less sweet if I had acted in a way that would have made disapproval from some less likely.

A Brief Encounter

In the first few months as a freshperson and a virgin, I met a lovely young woman whose company I enjoyed. We talked about many things, some in depth. There was much peer pressure to couple and have sex. We responded to that pressure by beginning to touch and kiss each other, which was pleasant, but at that critical juncture of truth, investment of self and possible conception, I remember saying something like, "I like you and enjoy being with you, and this (the physical contact) is very nice, and I'm attracted to you, but I just don't feel this way now, you know?" Hormones and desire may have been running too high at that moment, but I think she understood later.

Moral: Portray any image that is useful, but when push comes to shove and a critical moment where someone could get hurt (maybe you) is at hand--be extra sure you tell the truth to yourself, and about yourself--know what you want, and who the hell you are, and be honest about both. My future experiences in this realm did not always end without consummation, but I have tried to have them live or die in the light of honesty and truth about my feelings and intentions.

To Argue or Not To Argue

I took a class in Argumentation from a communications professor who also happened to be a local political candidate. He kept losing because he would not change his stand on abortion, he was pro-life. I respected him for that, even though I was pro-choice.

The format of the class was a series of graded debates. The class composition was me, one black male who looked like he'd just gotten out of prison, and ten suburban whites and two black females. We had to chose or be assigned a debating partner after our first speech which was suppose to convince the rest of the class of our viewpoint, and we were graded on class response combined

with the instructor's evaluation. The two black females let loose
like twin Angela Davis's, the black guy could hardly talk, but he
got off a few good one-liners, and the suburban whites were kind of
a cross between Ted Koppel, Sam Donaldson, and/or William F.
Buckley. I was the only a la Garrison Kellor of the bunch. The
suburban whites paired up, the Angela Davises got it together, and
by the professor's suggestion, I was paired with the black male,
who never came to any of our practice sessions together, and then
stopped coming to class on any kind of a regular basis, especially
when he and I were scheduled to debate. What surprised me about
all this was that the professor always welcomed him. He did not
have to put up with his delinquency for too long, since after awhile
he stopped coming to class altogether. Consequently, I did all my
debates alone, against two people on the other side.

Naturally curious about why he had allowed this, I went to the
professor's office during office hours to ask him why he had
assigned this person to me, and why he had put up with his
nonsense. He told me that he had perceived me as a person who
would not put up with any nonsense from the individual in
question (this was a good perception on his part, I did have it out
with this person once when he wanted to let me do all the research
and then show up for the debate--I refused to cooperate with him
under these conditions). We also discussed my speech delivery
style, he said I was too folksy and personal, that I needed to stand
straight and present my points more like a candidate running for
office (I tried this too, but could not carry it off because I could not
believe in it, and I could do some fairly effective things a la folksy

and personal, being two and one in debates as determined by student vote, while debating alone. I got a B plus in the course). I was very upset that this professor had clouded my academic experience and workload by not having enough guts to take the situation in hand, and instead handled it by letting things slide and doing nothing, which forced me to do the something he should have done himself--he said yes, that I was right and that he was sorry. Still upset at having all this supposably washed away by a few painless words from him, I told him, to his face, that he reminded me of a public relations man, slick with words, but without substance. He said that we both were what we were and could not apologize for that.

Moral: My first mistake in the area of psychological indenturement. At the point where he had apologize to me--I had him. If I would have showed my frustration in another way, perhaps by an exhausted look, or some comment, such as," well, I'm glad things eventually worked out," I would have indentured him unto me, and might have gotten an A minus or A in his subjective final evaluation, making what I had gone through more worth my while. As it ended, I gained little or nothing where I might have gained more.

A Chance to Gain

After receiving a test back which I had not done as well as I would have liked and wondered about some of the problems and how they were graded, I approached my chemistry professor to ask him how I might offer questions and appeals for changes concerning the test. There were several students at his desk doing more or less the same thing, and the mood was one of some levity. When I got a chance, I asked him what procedures I might go through to offer appeals concerning test questions. He had been talking to another student who was not as seriously bothered by their test performance, and turned to me without observing my mood and said with a smile," You could get down on your hands and knees, and beg, and cry and whimper and plead with me to have mercy on your poor mind," and from the look on my face and then the look on his and those other students around him, we all knew he had just offered insult to injury and had made a serious mistake.

I replied, with just the right non-challenging self-respecting tone in my voice," Well, I won't be doing any of those things." A few days later, this professor and I discussed this exchange, he said he was sorry, I said I knew he hadn't meant it the way it sounded, and to forget it. This professor ended up writing me a nice recommendation, and gave me an A minus in his course, a grade I earned via a second chance he offered the entire class on the final. Other contributing factors to this professor's goodwill towards me were attending the same church and having discussions about other topics he was interested in, like his hobbies and leisure activities.

Moral: My first unplanned exercise with psychological indenturement. I could have said many things to this professor in the form of an attack, but decided instead on self-respect and holding my ground as a student asking a teacher a reasonable question. This behavior got results in the form of a useful recommendation and a favored academic atmosphere. A potential did all I could to maintain his favor, and all he asked was that which any employer might ask of his employees. He did not berate employee, even when they made errors (like the day man did) and if he had to talk to you about an error that you had made, he did it in private, not in front of the other drivers (like the day man sometimes did even though he was told not to by his superiors). If you find an ally like this, do what you can to keep him your ally.

A Return on Behavior

A certain professor in a certain subject area changed my final grade from a B minus to a B. The final curve was very close, 81 and below being a C plus, 82 being a B minus and 83 being a B. My performance had steadily improved throughout the course. I went to this professor after the semester was over, disturbed by the B minus, and how it would affect my overall GPA, and that I wanted to make sure I had been graded correctly. I showed him my other grades from that semester, his B minus being the lowest one. We checked my actual score, it was an 82 point 4 something. He looked at my other grades, I had taken a heavy load that semester, and received three A, one A minus, one B plus, one B, and his B minus. Certainly he considered this, but moreso I believe he considered the attitude I showed toward learning and life. When I had come to his office before with questions on tests and homework problems, other students had been there too, often with the same problems. I was more inclined to listen to his explanation and easily see and admit my mistake or misperception and then correct it, others there were more inclined to argue with him. I was easier to teach than them. Also, this professor had seen me involved in community recreation activities, coaching kids, his own children involved in the program at another level. I had left a favorable impression. Consequently, it was easier for him to change my grade to a B.

Moral: If you can, observe and control the impression you make on others via image enhancement.

A Case for Reconnaissance

I was enrolled in an ethics class with a philosophy professor of world-class reputation. I wrote a seven page paper for his class. I did no reconnaissance on him at all. When I received the paper back, it had notes like "uh-huh," and "yes ok," and "I see" all through the margins, and at the bottom of the last page at the end of the paper the professor had written, "This is clear and well-argued, but I'm not sure what you are saying." He gave me a B plus for one part and an A minus for another part, and figured those two grades together somehow to produce a final grade of B plus on the paper. I never questioned him about his final comment, nor did reconnaissance on him, nor took another philosophy class after that, but I learned about the esoteric element in philosophical understanding and the subjective nature of grading--in spades. If I had done a paper on the same topic that was still clear and well-argued, and that he liked and subconsciously or consciously agreed with, I suspect it might have been clear and well-argued enough to receive a grade of A.

Moral: Do reconnaissance on professors, not only for image

enhancement, but also to slant your ideas advantageously in papers you will submit for their subjective approval. Do not worry about writing what you really think about the topic--you will discover keenly what that is as you write what it is not and can save those special perceptions for when you can present them with impunity and serious impact. If you can, write some of what you really think that you know the professor will like.

Sometimes You Cannot Be Friends

I met a chemistry professor of some professional stature who I genuinely liked and who also I believe, liked me, simply on a personal basis. I was doing fairly well in his chemistry class. It occurred to me to ask him for a recommendation, but I was hesitant to do so, because I thought he would think I was using our personal friendship solely for my own gain. However, I needed the recommendation. I was just getting to know him when I asked him for the recommendation. He said he would do it, but it changed our whole relationship. I could tell he was beginning to distance himself, once I even asked him about this. I told him it had not even occurred to me to ask him for a recommendation at first, I just thought he was an interesting guy, which was true, and he assured me he knew that, and it was ok. He wrote me a nice recommendation, but it bothered me that getting the recommendation seemed to cost me our budding relationship. Perhaps if I had not asked him for the recommendation, he would have taken me up on my offer to cut wood with him on his farm, or encouraged me to apply for work in his lab, or perhaps he would have eventually distanced himself anyway.

Moral: These are the fortunes of war, I guess. The situation left me with many unanswered questions. I don't know why we hit it off or why he distanced himself, maybe he was afraid I would ask him for more "professional" help than he wanted to give, or that I was lonely and would abuse him as a social outlet, or that I was really conning him into giving me help by pretending to genuinely like him. The saddest part of all this is that I was not pretending. After his distancing began, I use to fantasize that if the two of us were ranchhands on some old-time western range, we would have worked together well and enjoyed each others' company. The point of this story is to re-emphasis something I mentioned in Basic Concerns and Strategies--CHANCE. I was just lucky to meet this person, and, I guess, to get a good recommendation from him.

Parents as Enemies and Allies

There have been times when my parents, especially my father, have behaved as my enemies, for a limited time. Most of these occurrences have come out of not understanding me or the demands that college placed upon me. My father would promise to help me, he would promise to pay for certain things, but when the time came to do so he would often reverse field and ask me how I was going to pay for them. I came to know that if I told him, perchance, that I needed to cross the Atlantic he would say yes--he would finance it--and then send me a dinghy, minus the oars. Dad, I'd say, you said you would pay for it, and then would come the litany of his financial burdens, some of which were real, and he would ask me what I could realistically contribute, which was usually nothing since I had not planned on having to contribute, since he said he would pay for it. What he really meant when he said he would "pay for it" was that he would help me pay for it. This would not be an unrealistic expectation if it were accurately stated from the beginning. Maybe he liked the sound of his voice saying, "I'll pay for it," but his practice has lead to several misunderstandings which I have now learned to expect. Perhaps the reason he did it was because he thought one should work their way thru college, which is fine, but one must know the rules one plays under. He seemed to always underestimated what I would need to accomplish my purpose.

At age nineteen after three semesters of college I called him to tell him that I was quitting school because I was confused and did not know what I wanted to do with my life. He said, "Well if you do you'll get no help from me, you'll be on your own." He is an educator himself, he wanted me to stay in school, so he chose this tack. He also underestimated my dedication to my confusion, for I quit anyway. I found out what "on your own" means. It means riding one's bicycle twenty miles round trip each day, whether it snows or not, to wait tables. It means living in places with people who could kill you if they were having a bad day. This was really good for me, being confused already and then becoming somewhat desperate, exhausted and subconsciously afraid really helped me find direction in life (ha!). He had failed to understand my situation, I was not lazy or flunking out, I just did not know what I wanted. In my opinion, for all you future parents, he made this process harder than it had to be, at least for about six months, wherein he discovered that his methods were not getting the results he had thought they would, and he began to help me some. I got an old car, I paid for it, he helped me with insurance. I moved to a residence out of danger, he helped me with half of the rental deposit, and eventually, I went back to school when I was ready and was not confused anymore.

My father also told me that I would be foolish to pursue a writing career, and that the average writer does not make much of a living. He completely misunderstood my reasons for wanting to write, and either had no confidence in me just then or was trying to protect me from a life of poverty. My mother told me not to try to get into medical school again after I was not accepted the first time and if I did anyway, to be prepared not to get in. I felt like my most ardent supporter had just cashed in her chips. Ironically, my father told me to hang in there and try again, but offered no help in the interim, except to reiterate that if I got in he'd pay for it. Both of them were trying to protect me, I guess, and I can excuse and forgive all these little problems because things worked out ok, and I was the first-born, the experimental child, they have not made these kinds of mistakes with my siblings, in fact, as it must seem to many first-borns at one time or another, my siblings have had it seemingly easy in comparison.

Moral: ANYONE can be your enemy. And that person can change just as suddenly and be your ally. Get away from anyone who can effectively undermine your dreams before you have a chance to dream them fully, before you can even begin to build the foundations under your castles in the sky, even if those people are people you love dearly and cannot imagine living without--like parents.

Don't Ask Me, Admire Me

In a certain course, I perceived early in the semester that the professor wanted no nonsense, which included asking too many questions in class. To ask one question was ok, he liked that, but to follow that question up with another was risky, especially if that question challenged his previous answer. Unfortunately, he misspoke himself all to often, and gave incomplete or unreasonable answers while prodding us on with remarks like, "and that will be on the test," which made exercising restraint in asking questions about his misinformation very difficult. One woman, who I knew to be a superior student, found it impossible. She got into it with him more than once. I decided to try to ask, but if I did not get satisfaction on the first try, to smile and nod and pretend to understand.

He wasn't kidding when he said "it would be on the test." His tests were difficult, partly because he was so unclear, and partly because of the difficulty of the subject matter. I was friendly toward him, and when my scores on the tests did not equal the number marked wrong from the total possible points, scoring them instead to my advantage, I asked around to see what others were experiencing, and they too had noticed discrepancies. I got an A minus in the class. We had the option of dropping one test grade of four, and the one all savvy students want to drop is the final, they do not want to have to cram and relearn all that useless information again, everyone scrambles to do well on the three tests that come before, each easier to prepare for than the final because each covers more limited material. After the third test, there were moans and groans throughout the class, for some knew then that they would have to take the final if they wanted to get a decent grade. I was one of the lucky ones, but I still had a question about a question on the exam, and I went up to ask the professor about it. Ahead of me was the superior female student who had argue with him in class, and they were at it again, and I was privy to the conversation for long enough to tell that he thought she was doing badly in his course. In fact, he asked her point blank if that wasn't really why she was upset!   She said no, that she had gotten two A's on the first two tests, and on this one she got a little lower score, though still pretty good.   I asked my question, preprogrammed to be friendly no matter what his answer. Afterwards, I wondered how much his perception of a student affected their grade. There were discrepancies on some tests that could not be accounted for. I'd be very surprised if that superior female student didn't get an A in his class, since scoring was on an objective basis, but I wonder???

Moral: Even when you are graded on an objective basis, it is still important to "get along" with the professor, no matter how terrible a pedagogue he/she is, and no matter how much more than he/she you know about the topic. Image enhancement, one of docility and apt attention, with sporadic homage questioning, worked in this situation.   Critical analysis of lecture material presented and subsequent questioning, like that of the female student, may have made a bad impression, and may have affected her grade. When it comes to grades, you never know if there isn't some subjectivity mixed in with that supposed objectivity.

The Dating Game

In my physics lab, I had an attractive female TA who came from India. As the semester progressed, I came to sense that she was attracted to me, and would like to get to know me better, and though the idea has some appeal to me, I think she was more keen on the idea than I. Nevertheless, our relationship progressed through the semester, at one point near the end of it we almost went out, but I decided at the last, and told her so, that I thought we should wait till the end of the semester.

After the final grades were in (I got an A), we went on a date. Our dinner and our conversation in the restaurant went ok, but then we had to agree on which movie to see afterwards. Her command of English was good enough to handle physics, but not so complete that I thought it could grapple successfully with all nuances of fast-paced, verbal movie humor. For this reason, I thought she would enjoy Stevens Spielberg's Goonies more than Chevy Chase in Fletch. I thought the verbal pace of Goonies would be slower, and the humor more physical and slapstick, and that would allow me enough time to fill in the gaps during the movie, so that she could get the full, or nearly full intention of things. I told her, for these reasons, I thought we should see Goonies.

During dinner we had some words about the advantages and disadvantages or our respective countries of origin--she was somewhat pro-India as one might expect, and I played the role of U.S. advocate ever so gently. When I gave my reason for my choice of movie, it was as if I'd insulted her whole clan and nationhood, she insisted on seeing Fletch. "I can speak your English!" she insisted.

Never having been one to argue with a Brahman, I acquiesced quickly and painlessly. This point settle in my mind and won in hers, we proceeded merrily to the movie theater.

As I'd expected, the movie was fast-paced and full of witty double-entendres. She was lost after the first fifteen minutes, and the movie moved too fast, and the "shhh!" from others became so insistent, that I could not keep her informed about each and every little thing that was happening. After another ten minutes, I gave up. Ten minutes later she turned to me and said that she did not understand the movie, and that she had things to do in her lab, and then she got up and left. I stayed and enjoyed the movie, more glad that she was gone than insulted. It all turned out ok though. I never saw her again, and during dinner I had slipped back to where the waitress was preparing our order, and asked her for a date. She gave me her phone number and we went out the next weekend--but that is another story.

Moral: Never date your TA, or for that matter, your professor before the final grades come in. I wonder if this little incident had happened mid-semester if I would still have gotten an A in the class. One never knows, and as for dating TA's, it often turns out better than this, another one I dated from a music composition class (after the final grades were in) should still be dating me today, but alas, she was a better judge of character than I thought.

The Seduction

Once upon a time, in a cottage away from campus, a professor's wife sexually propositioned me. She was not unattractive, and he was an intelligent, virile, nice guy. As it happened, I had felt it coming on the other times I had met her, but thought I was mistaken, for though I knew their marriage to be somewhat unsatisfying for her, I did not think a little tumble was what she really wanted, even though it appeared that way. When she approached me, honestly and directly, I tried to remind her of all the special things she had with her husband and her family, and though I liked her I did not want to sleep with her no matter how much "fun" it might be.

Strangely enough, one never knows how one will respond in such situations, and I had not planned what I would say, but somehow it came out as I intended. She receive it reluctantly, but graciously. Months later, I saw her again, off and on. Happier and still married, she had gotten back into college teaching, and seemed to be enjoying her autonomy. Perhaps that is what she really wanted from her professor husband at the time, more respect for her intellectual autonomy, or who knows, maybe she'd taken a lover.

Moral: Never sleep with your professor's wife or husband. What could happen to you if he/she found out, even if your final grade was in, might be written about in romance novels with great flare, but is probably most unsavory, and who knows, what she probably wants is someone or something else anyway. Vengeance sought for sexual improprieties can have long arms. This experience, well beyond the dictates of strategies and image enhancement, is included just to illustrate how demanding certain "academic" situations can be, and what similar tests your judgement may face.

A Case of Unique Style

My first TA for second semester calculus had a "unique style" of teaching which it only took me till the review of our third homework assignment to loathe. He would read through and explain the examples that were already given in clear and excruciating detail in the text, usually taking almost all of the class time to do this, and then give us our next assignment. Most had already covered and understood these examples, and needed help with the more difficult, already attempted, previously assigned problems. When asked to work through these problems on the blackboard during class, he refused to do so. When I asked him why he would not do the problems for our edification, he explained that this was his "style" of teaching and that we should go to the math lab, which met a few afternoons per week in the mathematics library, if we had any questions. Suddenly, I knew I had a problem.

At the time that I realized that this TA was going to be a problem, the deadline for drop-add was only two days away. The first two assignment had been easy enough so that few of us had any questions, and had not experienced the ramifications of his "style." Even after he announced it, I thought I might be able to get enough help to do well in the course by using the math lab, until I tried to use it. Sometimes it was cancelled, sometimes I could not go at the time it met, sometimes the overloaded instructors were mobbed by other students, usually those from other classes who were having difficulty with the more fundamental concepts, and sometimes the instructor in the lab could not quite remember just how to do that one right that minute, explaining that he use to know, but had not worked with those kinds of problems for awhile. Trying to use the math lab to learn, I soon found out, was like trying to make ice cubes in hell. By this time, the first test was only two weeks away.

I decided to try to get help from the TA. Gently and in class, I asked him if he might consider amending his style some, and do a few examples from previous homework assignments in class, like other teachers do. My suggestion was met with mumbled agreement from the rest of the class. He dismissed this suggestion out of hand, maintaining his assertion that he had a right to teach in his own style. I told him of my problems with the math lab. This too was echo by the rest of the class. He remained unreformed. I tried to remind him, in no uncertain terms, that we were paying him to teach us, and that he had a certain responsibility to respond to our academic needs. He said that we could get those needs met in the math lab. I said we couldn't. He said we'd have to. End of discussion.

Immediately after class I went to the chairman of the

department and told him about all this. He said he would consider it. The next day he said I could transfer out of this TA's section after the first test.   Since I was the most vocal, I would be the only one allowed to do this. After sitting in on a few other TA's classes, I found one who happened to be a full professor who used a question and answer format with his classes, and who did very instructive examples of difficult problems in the text. I transferred out of the class as arranged.

Moral: I should have recognized this TA as an enemy sooner and taken appropriate action--dropping his section for another. Killing him with kindness or trying to influence his attitude toward me with image enhancement would have had limited application here, though I might have been able to make a more mellow transfer out of his section, and if trapped in the section, using appropriate image enhancement would have been the best response to the situation, short of strangling the TA in some dark alley. Maybe a more pleading, groveling performance in my request for help might have turned the tables, or perhaps enlisting the help of one of the females in the class to make the plea, for I believe he may have been more responsive to this coming from a woman, being himself a somewhat unattractive, homely man. As it turned out, hierarchy manipulation and some image enhancement, in making my case for the chairman of the department, were the solutions in this case.

Calculus was not my best subject, and besides seeing little use for it as a doctor, I was working part time while taking one other class, a chemistry class with a lab, but still I thought I could get at least a B or better in calculus, and was determined to do so. On the first test, from the TA with the "unique style," I got a C minus. In the second instructor's course I got an A on the second test, and a B on the third. These scores averaged out to a B minus, just below a B. I did not challenge the first TA on my reported test score, nor did I say another word in his class during my remaining time there after the transfer was arranged. My score was among the pack and the scores were low, so he may have been grading on a scale, instead of a curve, or perhaps he was using a vendetta. I should have challenged him on this grade, but to do so might have meant taking the time to go to an appeals committee, unless I could get him to change the grade on his own. That semester I just did not have the time to do this, though I should have at least tried to talk with him about it, and improve my position if I could. I suspect that I would not have made much headway with him, unless I threaten to talk with the chairman again, and even then he may have held firm--I did not try it, so I do not know for sure.

Intimidation versus Image Enhancement

In a vertebrate zoology lab, I was assigned a lab partner who seemed just fine at our first introduction, but soon became difficult to work with. The first day that we were cutting into our specimen, he told me all his grades from the previous semester in biological science, all of which were quite respectable, and then told me what he expected to get in our course. All the time he was doing this, he was also trying to assert that he was the brighter of the two of us and should take the lead in deciding how we should proceed with the dissection. I mention that I had passed freshman biology by examination, and let the issue of who was brighter pass, treating him with limited deference, and let him take the lead in the dissection of our specimen.

It soon became apparent that I had a gift for visualizing anatomical structures, besides being very interested in the subject, and that I was going to excel in this class, his previous performance notwithstanding. This established, we worked together quite well, sharing the dissection chores and access to the specimen cooperatively.

Moral: This person tried to use intimidation on me from the start. I, in turn, could have tried to intimidate him with any outstanding past performance, using anything from grades to sexual "conquests," real or mythical, as foolish people are apt to do, but instead decided to give him what he wanted, which was surrender on my part. He wanted a surrender that could only hurt my pride, and not my grade in the class, and if fact, it may have help it along. Intellectually, I ignored his attempts at intimidation from within the privacy of my own mind, and being pushed by him into that quiet, private retreat may have helped me to really focus and concentrate on the material. Not retaliating kept us from coming into conflict, so that we could continue to work together. The enhanced image used was one of surrender, and eventually, benevolent teacher, and it worked well. Intimidation versus Image enhancement: Image enhancement 1, intimidation 0 (and image enhancement does not require that one run the risk of doing undue psychological harm to the enemy, i.e., I did not psychologically interfere with his ability to perform in class, and, if anything, I was a help to him).

What Did You Say?

In a certain science course, I had a foreign TA who could hardly speak English. It did not take me long to realize that learning the topic from him would be next to impossible. I dropped the course immediately, opting to take it next semester from an instructor who I went out of my way to meet, and ask others about. He was described as moody, but at least he could speak English, and I would be able to understand him.

Moral: I recognized the foreign TA as a defacto enemy, he would hinder my learning and quite likely my performance. Image enhancement, unless I could learn his native tongue via Berlitz, would not help me change this situation, nor could hierarchical manipulation make him a better English speaker. I took appropriate action, finding someone I could learn from and use Image Enhancement with more effectively.

One Second-Hand Seersucker Suit

Early in my exposure to a new university, I had a chance to compare the locker room and athletic privileges accorded students versus faculty and staff. The faculty and staff had their own locker room, and each occupant was provided with his own locker, soap and towels, and any other athletic equipment, like shorts, supporters, shirts, socks, sweats, rackets, or basketballs etc. at request, or, depending on the equipment, with an exchange of an available annual pass, purchased at a reasonable rate. Students in physical education courses could get baskets, but they had to stand in line and wait for basketroom personnel to bring it to them each time they used it and had to fill out a form for each piece of equipment use over a semester. In addition, they had to exchange their pass each time they got their basket, and their privileges were limited by the semester they were enrolled in physical education classes. I did not even check to see what non-physical education students were provided, and since I did not intend to take any physical education courses, I knew I wanted a locker in the faculty-staff locker room, but was not sure how to get it. I certainly could not get on the faculty, so that left becoming a part of the university staff.

Just to see what identification was required, I visited the appropriate office where faculty-staff annual cards were purchased. Dressed well in a second-hand seersucker suit for previous job interview, I approached the appropriate window and asked for a faculty-staff annual card. The woman at the window pushed a short form through the grate which I proceeded to fill out, fabricating the position I held which was within the university system, but was not considered a staff position. One part of the form asked for a faculty-staff employee number, which I did not have. As I handed the form back, I told the woman at the window that I had just started my job, which was true, and did not know my number. She said that was ok, that I should just drop by and tell them when I knew. I paid the fee and got my faculty-staff card. The basketroom personnel gave me a locker and all the equipment I requested, not questioning a man with a new faculty-staff card dressed up spiffy in a seersucker suit. Five months later I attained a position which was staff eligible.

Moral: Image enhancement works! I took on the appearance of a professional and was accorded the privileges of a professional, even though I was a lowly student at the time. Upon approaching that window, pulling off a successful con was not my intention, though it had crossed my mind. It all just kind of fell into place, and I got and paid for privileges I was entitled to anyway--five months early.

The High Cost of Victory

In a certain course, a professor showed a film which contained viewpoints I thought were illogical, outmoded and obsolete. After the film was over, the professor asked if there were any questions. I asked, in a jocular way, "When was that film made?" She replied with a tirade of argument supporting the film's views, etching each point I was wondering about in our minds, and then giving her refutation. I could feel the murmurs in the class as she talked on, I was not the only one who had doubts, and she seemed intent on not confronting our doubts, but castigating them before they could be fully brought to our awareness, interpreted, articulated, and then brought to her attention. She did not want to discuss these views, nor did it seem she would even allow us to discuss it, even among ourselves, if it were within her power to exert enough mind control to prevent this from happening. At the end of her five minute response to my request for a copyright date, she said to me, "Now please tell me what you were implying with your question and any objections you may have."

"O none at all, ma'am," I replied sarcastically. The class broke into an uproar of laughter.

Moral: This was an incredibly stupid thing to do, though it felt so good at the time. I had dented this professor's armor publicly by getting a laugh at her expense. Wrong, wrong, wrong--even if I was right, it was wrong. Subsequently, I wrote a paper which I believe to this day was well-considered, serious, insightful and sensitive to the topic which was given a grade of B minus. I questioned her grade, we discussed it, we disagreed, my grade remained a B minus. In my opinion, this little episode in class did not help a favorable atmosphere for my discussion with her about the paper. Again, I thought of going to the appeals committee, but did not want to get involved in that long, drawn out, often fruitless process. I did no reconnaissance or image enhancement in this situation. I should have presented an entirely different image to this particular professor, but this was before my subsequent enlightenment.

The Paper Chase

Applying to medical school made me realize how important reconnaissance and image enhancement could be. Besides grades and MCAT scores, and recommendations, (the latter often a product of a good working understanding of the concepts mentioned in Special Concerns and Strategies) the rest of the process rests entirely on the impressions one makes in the interviews. I had several interviews, with several different interviewers, at several different medical schools. I had very little time to do reconnaissance on interviewers and schools in most cases, so I had to depend primarily on my observations of the interviewer at the time. Some of my interviews were bland and lifeless, others went extremely well. On occasions I was interviewed by a series of different people, or two people at once, and felt I had made a good impression on one or two of them, but failed to reach the third. Sometimes I thought the interviewer was tired of interviewing, and would be difficult to engage and to make a favorable impression upon, and sometimes it felt like they had already decide against you by their lack of interest. One cannot please all of the people all of the time, but each image you present must appear to be genuine to the observer. If you go overboard in the process of image enhancement and try to become something you are not, and get caught at it, kiss any good impression you might have hoped for good-bye. When in doubt, be yourself completely, rather than selectively. It is better to error on the side of honest disagreement, than to get caught in an act of fabrication. In the former, all they can do is disagree with you. In the latter, they can begin to believe you are not trustworthy, which is often the kiss of death in interview situations.

In my medical school interviews I tried to project my capacities to be insightful, and understanding of human nature, a quick study, caring, conscientious, a thorough thinker, perceptive, and kind, all with an appropriate sense of humor. Other capacities which I have which may in fact help me be a good doctor, but which interviewers, and people in general find unsettling are: being a free thinker; not getting caught up in the groupthink of a profession, a situation, or among colleages, a process in which others may find comfort for their lack of initiative, analysis, or compassion; being critical, or skeptical while in search of truth(s)-for the sake of not missing anything important; and being unyielding in the face of overwhelming peer pressure to change or conform in a way which I believe may harm others significantly. Medical schools want to mold their students to some degree, like so much putty, into tools of the profession. This is not all bad, but it isn't all good either-- and perhaps if I had showed some of these qualities I may not have matriculated.

Moral: Image Enhancement does not mean one should lie---it only means one should tiptoe around the truth for awhile, and see if the truth can be told without incurring any penalty or harm to one's self, or one's aspirations. In an interview, besides trying to make sure that the interviewer understands all your extensive credentials and experience and how they and you together can better serve their purpose, he/she must have a favorable impression of you as a person, which often boils down to if they like you or not, on some level. Look for topics and qualities that you and the interviewer share a mutual appreciation for, and stay in or stray into them ever so lightly.

These situations reinforce the need for a complete, thorough, ongoing Basic Concerns and Strategies so that one can work from oneself quickly and accurately (as if working from a familiar, favorite character in impromptu theater) to produce a favorable image, or if in doubt, to be oneself if one cannot get cues from observing the interviewer and decide on what might make a favorable impression.

Overdoing the Underdone

As a camp counselor at a summer camp, I came into conflict with the director over how the children ought to be treated. One of his methods was to have all the other children pile on top of an "offender." This was usually done at morning role call, initially at the director's whim, then later on a regular basis. The whole thing was meant to be fun, but sometimes the kids got carried away, and the whole experience became very frightening for the child who was at the bottom of the pile. I'd seen this happen a few times to a couple of campers in my cabin, and I happened to mention it to the director, but nothing changed, and the practice continued. I suggested he should find himself at the bottom of that pile sometime and see how it felt. He thought this would not be a good idea, since the kids might get out of control. It seems he sensed their animosity to his method.

Sometimes the counselors would be required to choose the morning's victim, and when it was my turn I called out the director's name, and before he could effectively veto the idea, the entire group of campers was headed his way. I had told some of the other counselors what I intended to do, and they and I were ready to wade into the group of campers to help the director, if need be. We let him get a good dose of his own medicine, then we waded into the pile of bodies and freed him. Afterwards, he was visibly upset, and this practice of "piling on" ceased.

Another time, the front end of the boy's waterfront dock was sinking, due to the diving board being there, and the constant pounding it took from young bodies at play. This same director, the waterfront director, and myself took a look at it. After our inspection, this same director decided we needed to reinforce the bottom of the lake with gravel, so that the legs of the dock would not sink. Upon further inspection, I noticed that the legs of the dock were expandable, all we needed to do was lengthen them via loosening and then tightening a few bolts. Both of these operations would be done in fifteen feet to seven feet of water, and would be somewhat difficult, but my idea was overruled by this director, and we proceeded to bring forth the gravel for seeding the lake bottom. During this operation, I was required to hold my breath, and squat and lift the dock in fifteen feet of water, while the director, wearing scuba gear, arranged the gravel underneath the legs of the dock. About the fifth or sixth time I did this, I was getting tired, and the dock had not risen an inch. Unable to coax me underwater as quickly as he wished, he decided if he could take the pressure off the legs by disassembling the dock, it might not sink so quickly when it came down on the gravel, and the gravel would be easier to seed. Soon we had five or six people in the water, all working to disassemble the dock. The situation was chaotic, and I tried to tell the director this but he would not listen. Suddenly, an eight by six board with nails sticking out of it shot out of the water with great force, just missing me and two others. The board had come from base of the dock and had been dislodged during its haphazard disassembly. At this point I told the director that I was not getting paid enough to take these kinds of risks, and that this was not in my job description, and that he was doing the job wrong, and then I went to shore. An hour later, two-thirds of the dock lay strewed about the water, and the director and his rag-tag crew had given up.

At lunch, this director, who directed the boy's side of a co-ed camp, consulted with his boss, the director and owner of the whole camp, about the dock problem. In its present condition the waterfront was unusable, except for the first twenty feet of water. The waterfront director told me as we were leaving the mess hall that the people who originally constructed the dock would be called, and that the waterfront could be out of commission for as long as two weeks.

I had a free hour and a half after lunch. I found another capable counselor who also had a free hour and a half, and an hour later, we were putting the last piece of dock together after having expanded the legs as I had suggested. Just then this same boy's side director, and the director for the whole camp happened down to inspect the dock. The owner was very pleased. The boy's side director wanted to know if there was just any little thing he could do to help. I said no, and the counselor enlisted for the task and I completed the reconstruction of the dock. Later, between sessions, when there were no children at the camp, I was fired by this same boy's camp director for "not wearing shoes after being on the waterfront."

Moral: Never show up your boss, or your professor, or anyone in power at or near the top of a hierarchy that you are near or at the bottom of, unless its a matter of life and death, or a point of the highest honor. At the time, the loss of this job was devastating to me, I really liked the kids and felt they liked me, which is why I believe I was terminated between sessions. I made no attempt at hierarchical manipulation in this case. I was so distraught over this minor setback, and others, at age nineteen, that I considered killing myself--to the point of loading a shotgun and putting it in my mouth briefly, then unloading it, checking twice to see that it really was unloaded, then putting the unloaded shotgun in my mouth again and pulling the trigger, click, and trying to imagine the transition from life to death.

Good use of Special Concerns and Strategy material with a correct choice of image enhancement could have prevented this entire unfortunate episode. To keep the job, I should have gotten along with this boy's side director's idiosyncrasies, and kept kids in the act of piling on from hurting or frightening the victim by wading in and removing bodies with a smile on my face, and gone along with him on his dock disaster, to the point of waiting the two weeks and keeping summer-crazed kids out of the water. At the time I just could not, but now, if I needed the job badly enough, I believe I could, right?..... (Naaaa!?)

The Power of Love

I met a young Jewish woman whom I fell in love with completely by accident. When I say by accident, I mean we became friends so naturally, I didn't notice it was happening, one day I woke up and I knew I loved her irrepressibly. If I'm not mistaken, I believe she had some similar feelings for me as well.

When in this process we began sharing with each other sexually I do not remember, but the feelings were there and growing throughout, as if this mammoth, unknown thing was there all the time, and I had not noticed it. When she told me she could not see me anymore, I got my first up close and personal lesson in race relations--Jewish families pressure their children to marry other Jews. At age twenty and coming from a place where I had not had much exposure to the finer points of Jewish culture, I was completely unaware of this.

It was so strange when she told me. Her face and body, were not saying what her words said. It seemed rehearsed. Neither of us could believe it. We slept together that night. When I met her mother, there was nothing I could do, short of being a Son of King David, that could please her. She did not hesitate to verbally abuse me and had to be restrained verbally by her husband. True to her parents urging, she tried to tell me again, and again, till she succeeded. My first love, an old story I'm sure, was over. I have always hoped that she too fell into this situation by accident, not having thought about whether she would hold herself to a tradition born of the struggle of her people. I have decided to believe that she was young and did not use me just to see what gentiles were like before returning to the fold. At the time, it was very difficult for me, and today, several years later, all I remember are the good times and the wonder of the love I felt for her, and with this memory, the love I have felt for others.

Moral: Certain areas in life do not lend themselves to the use of the material in Special Concerns and Strategies. Image enhancement would not have helped me here, because we had gone far beyond that, and I do not think being more cautious would have helped. These things happen, and they depress one, and that is their main danger. Be aware, after something like this happens to you, that this too will pass, and you need to give yourself time to hurt, to feel the pain, before you can fully heal. During this time, be nice to yourself. What did you learn about yourself and others? Love, when all is said and done, seems largely a learning process, we learn about many things by sharing with each other; how to get along with another, how deeply we can feel, and what a wonder it is to have love requited, if even for what seems a short, wondrous time. The important thing to realize after a loss like this is that you are at now in a weakened condition. You may not concentrate, study, nor plan as well as usual, and your image enhancement skills and others may be impaired. Before you venture on, as you eventually must, give yourself time to heal and gather yourself for struggles ahead.

Just Sex, Please

During summer school, I met a Mexican woman whose accent and manner I was very attracted to, and we began seeing each other regularly, the physical relationship evolving out of the passions of summer. As fall semester began, our class schedules became more demanding and we saw less of each other and one Saturday afternoon, after trying to see her for two weeks, I finally reached her on the telephone. We talked about the summer, and how much fun we had, and then about how it was becoming more difficult to see each other, and where our relationship was going. She said, in no uncertain terms, that our relationship could not be as it was, and that all she wanted between us was a mutually exclusive sexual relationship, that we would sleep together and have sex only with each other on a regular basis, with no thought of how our feelings for each other might influence the future: there would be no commitment. Though this proposal had its attractions, I told her that when I had exhausted the possibilities of finding someone who I could love, be loved by, and have a mutually satisfying sexual relationship with, I'd get back to her--and I never did.

Moral: This is an example of where someone misjudged me or men as a group, and should have used image enhancement or outright fraudulent representation, if anything, to be more sure that she would get what she wanted, which I can only assume was a sexual relationship without the risk of venereal disease. She could have feigned feelings for me and talked of a future together, and I would have followed her to hell and back, pouring my sexual energies into the relationship, all to her satisfaction. Eventually I would have seen the situation for what it was, but she certainly could have used me better, though it would have been extremely unkind for her to do so. There is a lesson within a lesson here, image enhancement has many applications and levels of practice, and it can be used on you as well as it can be used by you, and being aware of this should keep you on your toes as regards perceiving people in whom you place your faith and trust. One can also become involved in situations where the image one conceives and uses with a person is actually based on, and is a response to, an image that the person has presented, and so on, until nobody is really themselves, or even remembers what sharing themselves was about, though the situation itself may move along smoothly and without incident. (Scary isn't it?)

Ted and Josh

Ted and Josh were roommates and lived on my dormitory hall during my freshman year. Josh was from a very rural area of the country, and Ted was from New York City. Ted was very bright, a good writer, and charming person to be with, but had the notion that the way to have the diverse experiences of life necessary to write good fiction was to collect as many strange people as possible and bring them together in one place, and, if possible, get them high and wind them up with an argument over something unresolveable, and then let them go and observe them--especially if it had been a slow week and things were sluggish. Josh just came to school to get out of the rural area, to have some fun, and to get an education, in that order. Unfortunately for him, he was always a prime ingredient in Ted's staging of the actual experience of modern fiction. Drugs became more a part of Josh's life as they became more a part of Ted's human experimentation. My roommate also became a participant, along with anyone Ted could drag back to the dorm from the bar, no matter what the hour. Ted tried to enlist my participation, and I did to some extent, until I began to see the harmful affects it could cause, and how Ted did not care what those affects turned out to be. Last time I knew, Ted had graduated and was writing for a major city newspaper, and Josh had quit school off and on, and was driving a food delivery truck, still in the university town.

Moral: Professors, TA's, potential lovers and others are not the only ones who can be enemies, other students can undermine your objectives as well. You may have heard about students who sabotage each others experiments, and projects, but not about those who will provide you with a good time, and pretend to be your friend, but who really do not give a damn about you, and might be using you and your individual proclivities for their amusement. I think that to this day, Josh probably thinks of Ted as an old friend, someone he had some good times with, even though they were potentially destructive times for him. Josh could have used image enhancement to satiate Ted's desire to observe bizarre human behavior, and gotten along with him until he could get another living situation, and still achieved any objectives he might have chosen to set for himself. Perhaps Josh's problem was that he did not have very many objectives, or that they were swept into the background by Ted's charm, along with the lure of big city experiences and sophistications, and the constant availability and subsequent use of drugs. I wonder if Ted ever perceived what he might be doing to Josh. Strange to say, I hope not.

A Better Encounter

I met a special woman, we shared and taught and loved each other awhile, but I became sure I did not want her for a lifetime, though I decided I would like us to remain friends. I waited till she had no other pressures or stresses to deal with for a few days, and then I told her how I felt.

Moral: Image enhancement may be useful in the interim time one is waiting for the right time to tell someone news that could upset them. Pretending to like someone a little more deeply than you do, and supporting them in whatever they are doing, which often takes them away from you at the time, is not too high a price to pay, nor does it do them a disservice, as long as you tell them what is on your mind at an appropriate time. In the above situation, this feeling of, "Yes I like you, but this is not forever" was mutual, though sad nevertheless, and happily, we are still friends to this day.

Sacrificially at the Butt

In class, a guest speaker was having trouble making her points because the students did not want to choose the wrong option of the ones she'd offer, and become the butt of her example while she was allowed to triumph and make her point. The professor, after introducing the guest speaker, sat helplessly by and watched this drama unfold. As our guest speaker offered her second set of hypothetical choices to our abject silence, I met the professor's eyes briefly, then looked at the speaker as she dropped the choices in the form of a question into the laps of the students. There was a pregnant silence. I looked back at the professor, then back at the guest speaker who was waiting, and then back to the instructor as I raised my hand to become the sacrificial lamb. She called on me. I arbitrarily chose one of the possibilities she'd offered, replying in a calm, clear voice, and glancing at the professor as I did so. He smiled ever so slightly at me. I was wrong of course, and the guest speaker went on to explain why. She did not use this format for her next point.

Moral: Another example of psychological indenturement. I did not have to help this guest speaker's presentation along, and the professor knew that I did it only because I was trying to help her, and not because I thought I knew the answer to her question. In this way I was able to make a favorable impression on this professor.

Practice Makes Perfect

In a pet store, I once pretended to be the son of local kennel owner, and used my anger over how the animals were treated to make point about humane conditions for the animals. Dressed in a suit, I asked the clerk to give me a total on how much it would cost to buy a large number of saddest looking animals and after he produced the list, I threatened to call the Humane Society if something was not done. It was a complete bluff, the animals and I had nothing to lose, and they everything to gain.

On the phone, one can portray almost any image. Officialness and a soft voice that wreaks with subdued power can get one past all but the toughest secretary. People will tell a pollster things they would not tell their closest friends and family. Pretending to be a lawyer, or a law student investigating a case, or about to file a lawsuit, can get you loads of cooperation. On the telephone, if you know your stuff, and can think quickly, you can be anyone--

and get the results that your chosen image could easily reap. And remember--you can always hang up.

Moral: Chose a harmless situation that you can throw yourself into and try creating an image to accomplish some harmless purpose--it is good practice for the real thing.

In This Corner--Reconnaissance

About to take an advanced creative writing course, I did reconnaissance on the professor and found out he was very avant-garde, which I was not really into, being more Ibsenesque. For that semester, I pulled unfinished poems and writings from my writing files, "finished" them in the appropriate style, and used the time to work on my own writing projects, unmolested by this decent, though madcap and somewhat obtuse professor. I got an A in the course.

About to take a physics class, I checked to see which professor had the best reputation for teaching well among random students, and chose the professor who had the best teaching reputation. This particular professor was about to go on sabbatical, so I took the physics class sooner than I had planned. This decision paid off, for in a survey course where some topics are exciting and/or relevant to one's future, and others are not, and among a very competitive class of premedical students where receiving a B required one to score at or above the 86th percentile, I was able to get a B without taking the final, largely because this professor was a very good teacher and easy for me to understand.

Moral: Whenever possible, do reconnaissance on your

professors, and others in the hierarchy, do not depend on image enhancement alone. Doing reconnaissance can only enhance any subsequent image enhancement that becomes necessary.

Slow Down, Ya Move Too Fast

In an anthropology class, I became passionately enthusiastic about turning the developing, critical, analytical eyes of our class on the society that we lived in, rather than always confining our discussions to "them-type" societies, both primitive and modern, in which we were not participants. As I would ask how we were similar to those societies we were studying, the interest in the class diminished as the questions became more potentially revealing of our own mistaken notions and inadequacies, both collective and individual, but still I drove onward. Near the end of one particularly vigorous session of my questioning, a woman in the class became very upset by my relentlessness, and proceeded to make an ad hominem attack on me while making the point that these issues were not part of the course content. After the class, I talked with the instructor about this disagreement. Visibly upset, all he said was, "I saw it coming, I saw it coming."

Moral: Woe to he who tries to teach faster than some can learn. I knew I was upsetting some of my classmates with the questions I asked, but I did not stop because I thought they were relevant, and important. Chances are they were, but asking them was not worth the stigma, at least in this situation. If you find yourself in a similar situation, ask these kinds of potentially disturbing questions to yourself, unless you are ready to go public and face the possible wrath your questions may generate.

I got a B on the major paper in this class, and in the course. I wonder if I had been more cognizant of image enhancement if I might have receive a slightly higher grade, like a B plus, or an A minus, via the subjective opinion of the instructor who "saw it all coming," but took no active role in the happening.

Breaking and Entering for Grades

One time, I accidently left an important paper that was due that day with some other written material for a writing instructor who I knew well. I was about to leave the other written material with her personally, explaining that I could not stay long because I had to go turn in this other paper. She said she was on her way out too. I left the other written material for her critical eye in her cubicle office on her desk. Halfway out of the building I discovered that I had left the paper due that day with the other written material, and hurried back to her office to retrieve it. When I arrived her office door was locked, and her nearby cubicle dwellers said she would not be returning that day. Grabbing the top of the cubicle, I was able to pull myself up to see into her office, and see the material I had left for her, with the paper I needed, still on her desk. Explaining the situation, I asked her office mates if they had a key, they said they did not and I would have to wait for her return. "Well, I got to get in there," I said, and maybe I could just climb over the wall and get the paper and be gone. They, a vocal lot, said that if I did that they'd call campus security. Ignoring them, and calling their bluff, I quickly scrambled over the wall, wrote the instructor a brief note explaining why I was doing what I was presently doing, retrieved the paper, climbed back over the wall, and was gone; off to turn in the paper immediately before something else happened. I do not know if her office mates called campus security, but I never saw them.

That night I called the instructor at home to apologize for the disruption and intrusion, though I thought she would understand. My apology was met with peals of laughter. It happens that she did return to her cubicle office soon after I had left, and burst out laughing when she read my note, much to the chagrin of her colleagues. Apparently, she had been telling them they took themselves and their roles too seriously, and my little escapade and their reaction to it only served to dramatize her point.

Moral: Via thorough reconnaissance and good image enhancement, I had already made a favorable impression on this instructor. This "over-the-wall" situation only worked out because I knew the instructor well, and because I was desperate; if I had not turned the paper in that day it would have cost me some points and lowered my grade. Intuitively, though faced with vocal resistance, I knew things would be alright, because I knew the instructor trusted me and would understand, even if the campus police became involved. Part of the reason my action was ok, though risky, was because I had correctly estimated the character of the instructor.

Farmer Jones, Dumb Like A Fox

I had a job milking cows and doing farm chores. The work demanded a seven day work week, I had no days off and I lived on the farm with the farmer's mother in a house down the road from his. Because of this, I sought another job and received an offer to be a lifeguard at the YMCA. Ten days before the job was to start, I got notified that I was hired. This was at noon, when we'd taken a break for lunch. As soon as we got back to work, I told the farmer that I was going to take another job in ten days and that I would stay on until he found someone else. He said fine, and we worked hard that day. After the day's chores were done, and I had finished cleaning out the milking parlor, and was about to fill the grain bins that the cows would eat from while being milked the next morning, the farmer came roaring in, told me I was a lousy worker, and that I was fired. He wanted to take the buckets full of grain I had in each hand that I was about to fill the grain bins with. I told him I would do it, and that I could not believe what he'd just said. He hesitated a moment, not sure of himself or what to do, as I started up the ladder to the grain bins. Halfway up, he reached up and took the buckets from me and told me to go into his mother's house and start packing.

I went in and packed my things. His mother, whom had grown fond of me, and I of her, asked me what I was doing. I told her the whole story. When her son came in to see how I was coming and to settle up with me, she gave him one hell of a fuss, until I came downstairs and told her that this thing was between me and him. He paid me, I said good-bye to her, and I left.

Moral: I had completely misperceived this farmer. In a sense, he used image enhancement on me. During the day we worked together, he was his usual self, and did not complain about the work I was doing, though inside he may have been seething over the fact that I was quitting him. Perhaps I should have waited till I was ready to leave before telling him I was quitting, but I wanted to give him a chance to get someone else. When he fired me, I felt he'd had to work himself up to it.

When his mother got involved, I probably could have kept the job if I'd have wanted to, she being a force about the farm and very persuasive. I did not want to keep the job, I wanted to get out of there, and I wanted to leave while the going was good, and while the farmer still thought it was his idea. The old fashion image of man-to-man hunkerin' down and settling things worked well to diffuse the situation between the farmer and his mother, and I got what I wanted.

Mr. Thomas

I met Mr. Thomas in the men's shower in the faculty-staff locker room. He was an elderly man, and had retired from the admissions office at the university. He died a year and a half later. In the time I knew him he was always friendly to me, only tried to seduce me once, and was still friendly after I refused his sexual advances. He was a kind fellow, and loved to put his hand around the back of my neck and pull me to his shoulder. We took a few day trips together, he knew all the sites to see and the best restaurants, and had money to burn. I was his companion for a brief time, and though I did not like some of his habits, we had some good times together. He was a lonely old man with everything one might want in life, except love and companionship.

Moral: Nothing can buy love, not money, ingratiating behavior, sexual favors--nothing. Image enhancement cannot make love come your way, and it is a lousy pretext to love someone from, or because their image attracts. Mr. Thomas had become a master of image enhancement to protect his secret sexual preference, first as a career navy man, then as an admissions official at the university, and high-ranking officer in the campus ROTC program. By most measures, he had attained success, and perhaps knew love in his lifetime, though I suspect for most of his life he was very lonely, as he spent the last years of his life alone and died lonely.

Mr. Longstocking

Another locker room buddy, Mr. Longstocking was and is an active professor. We became friends. We went to baseball games, and to a secret skinny-dipping swimming hole together. Every once in awhile Mr. Longstocking would say something overtly suggestive of an interest in homosexuality, and I would ignore him, and when he talked about women in a sexual way, his descriptions were of conquest and performance. He once told me, "You know, I like you because we can talk about anything, nothing seems to phase you, you just accept it."

This was true for both of us until one candid discussion of his homosexual fantasies in the context of why he did not share more of himself with women and other equals, and how he seemed to prefer the company of students because they were "below" him, and usually would not have the insight nor the audacity to question him, and he could keep them at a reasonable distance from himself, and easily maintain this distance while finding some human warmth. We were discussing our relationships in general, how the condition I've just described, if they were an accurate statement of things, might be affecting his life, and the lives of others. As I left his house that night he seemed somewhat strained, and said, "Goodnight friend" with a pat on my back and a big smile on his face as I left.

The next time I talked with him, he said our discussion had "overstepped the bonds of our friendship" and I replied that I thought his problem was that he was raised before Vatican Two, and that he was a little too "variable" for me to be friends with. The next time I saw him in public, he was the same easygoing, smiling person who had said, "Goodnight friend" through his smiling, clenched teeth.

Moral: It seems to me that this man had been a mere image of himself for most of his adult life. When I knew him he'd just published a book, a critique in his subject area. Oddly enough, he wrote me a recommendation, and supported me when I had doubts about my future possibilities. We had both been images for each other, though I thought we were moving toward less image portrayal in our relationship, and more genuineness. Luckily, he was not grading me in anything and I had already attained his written recommendation, via some skillful image enhancement on my part, before I found our relationship unable to bear greater sharing and honesty, via his inability to break the habits of a lifetime. Strangely enough, I do not think this man was a latent homosexual, he simply was unable to show his quiet, gentle, sensitive nature to the extent it was within him, to men and woman alike, because he may have thought they would see this as unmanly, and perhaps feminine or homosexual-like behavior.

Psychological Honesty

I helped a PH.d psychologist friend of mine face his homosexuality by taking him out on a dark country road late at night, holding his hand, and asking him point blank if he often had homosexual feelings. He said he did, though he'd never acted on them, and wanted me to sleep with him. I told him that, though I could sense this feeling within him, I did not feel this way myself, and that he should find someone who could share his feelings and his passions.

Initially, I had great trepidation about confronting him with what I thought was the truth, since I wondered if him being what he was would condemn him to a life of unhappiness, but decided that this possible unhappiness could not be worse than living a life not being what one thinks and feels one is. After several experiments, he found a lover whom he lived with for five years before they parted. As I watched and shared as a friend in his relationships, I could not see much difference in the feelings that were involved if the relationships had been heterosexual. Heterosexuals and homosexuals can have enduring monogamous relationships. Heterosexuals and homosexuals experiment and fail. Heterosexuals break up and come together in the soup of all the same feelings that affect homosexuals, it is simply the expression of these feelings which is physically different. Only the preference and appeal of different forms of sexual expression make people homosexual, heterosexual, bisexual, or otherwise. The feelings involved, or lack thereof, are much the same. As the current AIDS epidemic sweeps across the United States and the world, affecting both homosexuals and heterosexuals, let us not forget that as regards our feelings as human beings we are all much the same and therefore bound together in this and every struggle we may face.

In my friendship with this particular person, there has always been a psychological honesty that we have shared and that I have come to appreciate even more as I sometimes seem surrounded by so many who are lacking this quality.

Moral: Be an image to protect yourself in potentially threatening situations, but face yourself on important issues and know who you really are, even if you have to hid it from certain, callous people who would not understand if you told them. At least in the privacy of your own mind, face yourself, and come to know the wonder that is you (see Basic Concerns and Strategies).

Not For Men Only

A woman I was lucky enough to meet became my friend and then my lover, and then my friend again. She was very logical and analytical, and loved to have philosophical discussions, and it was this mutual enjoyment that brought us together at first. Gradually as she shared her thoughts with me, she would repeatedly refer to parts of her female body as "useless appendages" and swore that she had no desire, nor skills necessary, to become a mother. Besides a slight weight problem, I also noticed that she had a penchant for leadership roles, and sought them out whenever possible, and was often awarded them, above many men who also desired the positions. To my surprise, I found out she was having some difficulty in school, and was on academic probation. Knowing her to be intelligent, I was somewhat shocked by this.

Gradually, as I was coming to know the aforementioned information, she and I were moving closer towards possible sexual union, but every time we might be getting close, she would pull away. Eventually we did share sexually with each other, and I learned why she had been so shy, and why she was the way she was.

The man who she gave her virginity too was physically rough in his performance of the act, and she had not enjoyed this. Afterwards, he was somewhat emotionally withdrawn, and this she took as a rejection of her as a woman. Feeling less womanly, she decided to try to excel in other areas, to be in command and in control, and to ignore her sexuality, and femininity. Fortunately, or unfortunately, her mind would not fully cooperate with her intentions, and this was affecting her ability to concentrate on her studies. As we slept together a few more times, she was able to find greater enjoyment in the sexual act. Unfortunately, or fortunately, she also became pregnant. Together we discussed our options, and together, though respecting the sanctity of human life, and wondering what a child created between us would be like, we decided on abortion because we knew we were not ready to be parents, and that if we did become parents we would not be able to give up the baby. It was done in the seventh week, and I was with her during the procedure, and took care of her afterwards. Because I wanted to get the full measure of what I was doing, I asked the doctor if I could see the tissue that had been removed from her uterus. It was not the arms and legs one sees in pro-life advertisements, and I would learn later in medical embryology class, that the fetus was developmentally at about the level of a fish at the time it was taken from her womb.

The whole experience changed her. Having that life inside her, even for awhile, lead her to consider the prospect of motherhood from a new perspective. There was something warm, good and nice about it, she thought, though she still had her doubts about her capacities as a mother.   Months afterwards, we were holding each other in the dark when she said she had to tell me something. She had slept with a man we both knew named Jeffrey while I had been away for the weekend.

The mixture of feelings I felt was profound. I liked Jeffrey. I cared for her, and knew that this was a milestone for her. For the first time, she had chosen a man instead of a man choosing her. She had seduce old Jeffrey, and it was important that she do so. I thought about what I knew about Jeffery and approved of her choice.   I also thought about how I cared for her--and I let her go to pursue her encounter with Jeffrey.

She and Jeffrey lasted about seven months, she was hurt when he left, but survived. Currently, she and Jeff are on opposite U.S. coasts, being apart for several years, and she has a new serious relationship, a fellow she met in one of her graduate philosophy classes while pursuing a degree in philosophy and international studies (she speaks several languages and did a stint in the Peace Corps). She is also somewhat slimmer, having lost some weight. Through all this she learned that being a leader may not necessarily preclude her finding pleasure and fulfillment in also being a wife or lover, and maybe a mother as well.

Moral: Men are not the only gender able to refuse delivery on their true individual natures when it is contrary to popular, and useful, trends and images that they may find pragmatic and/or currently in vogue. Ditto the previously mentioned notion that you should know your individual self, apart from the images you may use in the roles you may play, whether you be male or female.

Calmness Wins

A woman in a dormitory-style cooperative living situation that I happened to be house president of complained that one of the male members was making unsolicited sexual advances to her that she had indicated she was not interested in, but still he continued to harass her. She said she was afraid of him. She wanted him evicted.

To evict someone called for a house meeting at which two-thirds of the house voted to evict the offending member. I had run one other eviction hearing that year for non-payment of rent which had ended in a nearly unanimous vote for eviction, but this was second situation was completely different. The guy thought she was kidding, but she was not, and to make matters worse, the girl was not exactly the Virgin Mary. In fact, she had solicited me and one other male house member, but we had indicated that we were not inclined to be inclined. This woman was able to rally the support of the majority of the house members, who each notified me that they wanted a meeting on this issue.

At the meeting, I tried to make sure that all opinions got heard in equal measure. She told her story, he told his, she seemed like the innocent girl lost and breathless, and looking for help, he came across brash, bold and masculine, insisting that she had appeared in front of him with less than a formal gown on, attempting to draw attention to herself. He raised his voice and got excited in his explanation, she did not, but spoke in quiet helpless tones. The final vote was 12 to 6 for eviction (there were twenty member, the two members involved did not vote). I had to tell him he was out. Neither of us could believe it, and though I was relieved the situation had reached some resolution, I was not happy with the result, nor did I think it was fair. He was out within the two weeks he was given.

Moral: Sometimes people reach conclusions about you based on the image you present, and these conclusions may have far-reaching implications in your life. If he had not gotten excited and been very calm, and apologized for any misunderstanding, and shown no attraction to her at all in the form of his protest, even if he was in fact guilty, I doubt if he would have been evicted. Her performance, a helpless woman in trouble, was just what was required given the circumstances. After this meeting, many of those who voted for eviction had misgivings, but wanted to avoid any trouble in the future, and besides, he did seem a little excitable, didn't he?

Elementary Mistakes

I was terminated as a ward clerk in the hospital for wearing blue jeans to work. Other people in my position who trained me wore blue jeans, even though there was a written dress code prohibiting the practice. I had not seen the dress code, and blue jeans were not the real reason. The real reason was that I had turned down the casual advances of a nurse supervisor who documented my wearing blue jeans (I'd been wearing them about once a week for two months at this point) and had asked another nurse for a date. When the "scorned" nurse supervisor found this out, she sent a five item list of complaints about me to my supervisor, all pretext, the last being "called a nurse late at night and bothered her." I had called this nurse late at night, but with her permission after I was at home and she was at home, and a week after that phone call, this nurse called me and asked me for a date. In the interim, the "scorned" nurse supervisor had fired off the note. This all happened in December, I was not terminated until February. At my termination, I asked for a grace period in which to expand my wardrobe, this was disallowed. The offending female employees were given a grace period of three months to accommodate their wardrobes.

Moral: I had failed to note the extent of the power hierarchy. My supervisor, who dismissed the note from the nurse supervisor, was under the supervision of nursing. The "scorned" nurse supervisor was under the supervision of another nurse supervisor, and she under the supervision of yet another supervisor. All three played a role in my dismissal. If I had noted their importance and had been aware of the power they had, I might have played this situation differently, doing an image enhancement that would have taken into account all three of them. As it was, I only responded to my immediate supervisor.

All of the other clerks who supervised me and wore blue jeans were female. All the supervisors, including my immediate supervisor, were female. One might think I'd have a case for sexual harassment based on disparagent treatment (the lawsuit was filed, but do to lack of funds was not carried to completion).

Sounds of the Night

This is a true story. One night as I lay in my bed, while living in the dormitory-style co-op, I began to hear strange sounds coming out of the silence. Slowly it built to crescendo, a group symphony of expressed passion and love, loneliness for the moment begone. Since my bed was placed near the ceiling on a loft, I first heard the first voice from overhead. It went reke, reke, reke, reke, reke, reke, rekerekerekerek.... rekerekereke.. reke.. rekerekeREKEREKErekerekerekerekerekerekere, as fast as the springs of the bedroom instrument could keep up. It was Nanci overhead and her in-town boyfriend who came over on the weekends she did not go home to see her at-home boyfriend. Under the rise and fall of this leading voice could be heard the second voice, played on the same instrument by different players, from across the hall, a more legato-- rekerekereke, rekerekerekerekerekereke, reke, reke,.... reke..... rekerekereke .... rekereke that seemed to say, "just you and me babe," from a couple of overweight lovers who did not have anyone else and who had grown happy over their few years together, and then I heard a third smaller voice, a young, engaged to be married couple in the room next to mine- reke, reke, rekerekereke, reke re...ke,   re....ke, rekerekereke,   re....ke, re...........ke, rekereke, re.........ke, a softer, far different tempo, betrothed and committed to each other, fresh in love. I was sad I could not offer a fourth to this spontaneous composition, for I had the instruments, and the inclination, but alas, not the scored music of two hearts to follow.

Moral: No real moral here, except to say---I wonder what many images were at work and play that night?

On campus I have met and you will meet the many expectations of parents, professors, bosses, interviewers and lovers--both those on the way into your heart and those on their way out-- and when their expectations are not yours, or even if they are and you do not want them to know this, you can deal with them effectively, without necessarily losing their favor or incurring their wrath, by using the methods I have outlined.

FINAL REMARKS

Remember your objective(s). You are now ready for actual academic conflict situations, and believe me, they are ready for you. Acknowledge the need for self-reliance, and know your objectives. What have I told you to do? To not share all of yourself immediately, but to do so selectively, to not tell the whole truth(s) all the time unless you can do so with impunity, but to try to know the whole truth(s). To respond to attempted manipulation and exploitation by others using perception, judgement, self-control, and a selective, enhanced image to protect yourself. I have tried to convince you of the necessity of being yourself within yourself and how to defend that evolving self against ad hominem attacks directed at undermining or destroying your spirit to carry on, and to do so without malice towards or dehumanizing your enemies, and in self-defense, to struggle on and reach your objectives.

To some of you, it may seem like insanity to pretend to be less than all of yourself in order to have the space necessary to become yourself. I agree, it is insanity, but often if you are yourself, forthright and outward, you will be crushed by the many faces of power and authority that exist in our society before you have had a chance to begin to attain all that you might have been. Gradually, you will develop the ideas and achieve the means to emerge. Patience, a thing the young are sometimes short on, and often confuse with indecision, reticence, conformism or apathy, will be needed in ample measure, and more will be required of you than the simple honesty of being and becoming yourself, though that is the real objective. You must know when the conditions exist wherein that self, YOU, can survive and prosper. There will be unwarranted risks and foolish gambles, and you will make mistakes, and you will learn from these mistakes how to survive and to prosper--or, at some level, you will ultimately perish.

You cannot succeed all by yourself, but much of the time you will feel alone. Because you are alone: not only in birth and in death, but through much of your life. The perfect mate, the perfect friend(s), we hope for them, but they often do not materialize, ever yet, we cling to our hope. Many of us find comfort in God(s), whether real or imagined. There will be people we meet and know, they will help us and we will help them. Some of them we will call ally and some of them we may call friend.

Who are these special people we call friend? They are more than allies. They are rare. You will define them. Lovers too. They may be few and far between. Enjoy both while you may, for you may find that they are the real treasure to be gained in a lifetime: don't let your journey from romantic idealist to pragmatic realist via the pressures of competition and life inhibit your feelings, or your pleasures.

Finally, we have come full circle. Only you can know if you are ready. Come to know who you are and what you want, and tell yourself the truth(s). Remember your objective(s). Good Luck.

INDEX